The Biblical Mothers Deliver

The Biblical Mothers Deliver

The Chosen, the Saved, and the Disavowed

NANCY KLANCHER

CASCADE *Books* • Eugene, Oregon

THE BIBLICAL MOTHERS DELIVER
The Chosen, the Saved, and the Disavowed

Cascade Books
An Imprint of Wipf and Stock Publishers
199 W. 8th Ave., Suite 3
Eugene, OR 97401

www.wipfandstock.com

PAPERBACK ISBN: 978-1-6667-3347-1
HARDCOVER ISBN: 978-1-6667-2907-8
EBOOK ISBN: 978-1-6667-2909-2

Cataloguing-in-Publication data:

Names: Klancher, Nancy, author.

Title: The biblical mothers deliver : the chosen, the saved, and the disavowed / Nancy Klancher.

Description: Eugene, OR: Cascade Books, 2022 | Includes bibliographical references.

Identifiers: ISBN 978-1-6667-3347-1 (paperback) | ISBN 978-1-6667-2907-8 (hardcover) | ISBN 978-1-6667-2909-2 (ebook)

Subjects: LCSH: Bible—Feminist criticism. | Mothers in the Bible. | Motherhood in popular culture.

Classification: BS579.M65 K50 2022 (paperback) | BS579 (ebook)

12/07/22

For Leslie

Contents

Permissions

Brill Publishers has graciously granted permission for the republication of arguments and textual analyses found in chapters 3 and 6 of this book, portions of which appeared in a chapter I authored for a Festschrift for Dale Allison, entitled "Conceiving the Elect: The Virgin, The Matriarchs, and the God of the Womb" in *"To Recover What Has Been Lost": Essays on Eschatology, Intertextuality, and Reception History in Honor of Dale C. Allison Jr.* Leiden: Brill, November 2020.

"Phenomenal Woman" from AND STILL I RISE: A BOOK OF POEMS by Maya Angelou, copyright © 1978 by Maya Angelou. Used by permission of Random House, an imprint and division of Penguin Random House LLC. All rights reserved.

"The Christmas Poem" by Kaitlin Hardy Shetler. Used by permission of Kaitlin Hardy Shetler.

Copyright © 1981, 1993 by Donna Kate Rushin. Published in THIS BRIDGE CALLED MY BACK: WRITINGS BY RADICAL WOMEN OF COLOR, Fourth Edition (SUNY Press, 2015). A version of this work appeared in HOME GIRLS: A BLACK FEMINIST ANTHOLOGY (Kitchen Table Press, 1983). By permission of Stuart Bernstein Representation for Artists, New York, NY and protected by the Copyright Laws of the United States. All rights reserved. The printing, copying, redistribution, or retransmission of this Content without express permission is prohibited.

"Black Mother Woman". Copyright © 1973 by Audre Lorde, from THE COLLECTED POEMS OF AUDRE LORDE by Audre Lorde. Used by permission of W. W. Norton & Company, Inc.

Acknowledgments

My heartfelt thanks go to friends and colleagues who took the time to read through this experiment in writing for a general audience. Dale Allison, Jen Babcock, Barbara Belcher-Timme, Molly Childers, Leslie Grant, Anna Marslen-Wilson, and Laura Yordy all gave much-needed feedback on the nuances of a less formal tone, as well as the need for greater clarity in important places in the argument.

I thank Vickie Montigaud-Green, research support librarian at Bridgewater College, for the endless hours she saved me procuring the editions I needed of ancient source texts.

My sister, Leslie Grant, was my dearest ally and supporter as she read every page of this book in multiple iterations with energy and insight. Her encouragement of my work has been a constant gift to me, not just with this project, but for many years. The themes in this book are important to us both. I am so grateful to have such a generous sister and comrade in this life.

How Do We Read Stories That Reach across Millennia?

This book has grown out of my experiences as a mother, grandmother, and professor of biblical and interfaith studies. These three identities have complemented each other well over the years. I spend my days with students, nurturing their intellectual growth and helping them discover their relationship to a variety of religious traditions and worldviews in much the same way that I have done with my own daughters and granddaughter. I want them to discover who they are and the cultures that they come from. I teach them to respect all people, genders, and religions. I hope they will change the world for the better, in small as well as significant ways. I try to help them be free from fear and hatred, and to seek the same freedom for others.

In that spirit, I write this book about mothers in the Hebrew Bible ("the Old Testament") and their descendant-daughter Mary, who generations later becomes the mother of Jesus in the New Testament. Their stories teach us the intimacy and complexity of sexuality, desire, conception and birthing, family, betrayals, and the exiling of those who were once held dear. I have chosen to focus on the mothers' stories because I am interested in how motherhood defines differences between peoples in the Bible and today. Motherhood is the origin upon which all relationships are based. The mother's body is the only place where two human beings exist as one. It is the first place of belonging and shared identity, and eventually, also, of separation and differentiation from loved ones and "Others." Motherhood teaches us the intimacy, pain, and impermanence of relationships, as the processes of identity formation and individuation run their course.

The stories about the biblical mothers are ancient, but they speak of relationships like those we have today, good and bad relationships, not just between mother and child, but also across religion, gender, and ethnicity. The current traumas, divisions, violence, and pain that we as a culture are experiencing today also focus on sexuality and gender, as well as inter-ethnic ignorance, fear, and hatred. There is a relationship between these current issues and the ancient stories we find in the Hebrew Bible and New Testament. The biblical narratives of mothers who birth peoples created powerful arguments about national, religious, and moral difference, which have been handed down, told and retold, and applied across the centuries in ways that have created divisive social legacies.

These biblical stories are certainly not the only stories that have influenced our current cultural antagonisms, but they are powerful ones, and they are the subject of this book. All cultures hand down such stories. Perhaps looking again at the stories about the biblical mothers might help us see ourselves more clearly and understand better the inherited rationales and relationships that we take for granted, because they are driving us apart. The anxious and painful human experiences that the mothers' stories describe endure. The ways they have been told, retold, used, and abused over the centuries continues to cause loss, despair, and division. To read them again with this in mind is to study how the biblical mothers and their children became "us" and "them" and how we, too, have become "us" and "them." We are the stories we tell ourselves.

This is a book about stories, then, not history—biblical stories that describe relationships between mothers and their children, families, outsiders, and enemies. It is not about what may have really happened, but rather about how the mothers' stories have given birth to hopes, ideals, group belonging, fears, betrayals, desperation, belief in miracles, kings, messiahs, and even a god made flesh. So, who are these mothers?

In the book of Genesis, the matriarchs of Abraham's family, Sarah, Rebecca, Leah, Rachel, Zilpah, and Bilhah, give birth to the nation of Israel. The Hebrew Bible also gives us Lot's nameless daughters, as well as important "foreign" mothers: Rahab the prostitute, Tamar the Canaanite, and Ruth the Moabite. Lot's daughters, Tamar, and Ruth are instrumental in producing Israel's "golden boy" and messiah-king, David, who ruled at the height of Israelite power. From the New Testament, we have the Virgin Mary of the Christian tradition who is understood, at least by some early Christians, to be the mother of God. Through her son, Jesus, she helped create a new elect people who called themselves "the new Israel." Thus, mothers, sons, kings, messiahs, and peoples are all connected in these stories.

We too have mother-stories today, equally powerful, idealistic, and dangerous. It's important, then, to set the portraits of the biblical mothers side by side with current ideas about motherhood, gender, sexuality, and ethnicity. Indeed, comparing such ideas from the past and the present is natural. Most readers have gut reactions to the way women and men are described in books and stories, before they even think about what culture or time they may come from.

Wondering about influence—how past stories have influenced present ideas—is also natural. This book explores precisely such apparent influences as legacies of the mothers' stories in our culture today. Yet the question of influence is not as simple as it seems. For instance, biblical stories have not been absorbed or responded to in just one way by everyone—not in a single society, much less across cultures, not in any given period, and certainly not across history. Even the way the biblical stories were created is hard to pin down. Scholars think the stories in Genesis began to be written down centuries after the events they describe. After that, the Bible did not reach its current form until the turn of the millennium, around the first century CE. That is roughly a thousand years of stories, told and retold, edited, one book commenting on an earlier book, by many different authors in different parts of Palestine, at different stages in the evolution of Israel.

Israel began between 1200 and 1000 BCE as an ancient, small ethnic group, rural and isolated in the Palestinian highlands, then grew to be the wealthy and powerful nation of Israel centered in the city of Jerusalem around 1000 BCE, only to be defeated and exiled by surrounding empires later in the eighth to sixth centuries BCE. By the time the New Testament was written, the Israelites were known as Judeans, a divided and occupied people in first-century Judea, hoping upon hope for God to intervene and bring about a new age and restore Israel to its former glory. I ask you, how could stories passed down amidst all that transformation represent one single message about sexuality, mothers, God, families, and enemies?

The biblical stories themselves should be seen, then, as a "conversation" about these questions with no simple or universal answers. Together, they create an ongoing exploration of mothers and the peoples they birth, not always drawing the same conclusions. This makes their relationship to current cultural "conversations" and crises substantially more complex and helps explain why they have inspired such diverse values and behaviors in readers of the Bible.

It is clear that the Bible has always been, and remains, an immensely influential cultural force, however difficult it may be to simplify what its influence is. In my field of study, many biblical scholars disapprove of asking twenty-first-century questions or applying twenty-first-century morality about twenty-first-century cultural issues to biblical stories. Biblical texts, they argue, come from a different world and their original meanings can never be completely clear to readers today. Such scholars are not wrong, but the question of how the Bible's stories *affect* current cultural ideals, behaviors, and beliefs today—indeed, how they have done so over the centuries since they were written—is different than the question of what the stories *originally meant*. The fact is, their effects on the people who read them cannot be controlled by scholarly interventions, as valuable as scholarship is. Hearing and reading stories is always an intimate and ongoing act of interpretation. Readers of the Bible are no different. They understand what they read according to what they already know and believe. They understand according to their individual frame of reference, and/or that of the group they belong to.

For instance, today, as in the past, many use the Hebrew Bible and the New Testament as guidebooks for what they see as righteous and faithful living. For them, the patriarchs and matriarchs of the Hebrew Bible, the Virgin Mary, the apostle Paul, and Jesus are all models of how to be righteous and honor God—for how to live their lives today. However, what precisely that influence *is* depends on who is reading. Whether this is good or bad, subjective interpretations are a demonstrable reality, crystal clear in the never-ending disagreements about biblical teachings. Women, bodies, sexuality, wombs, and dysfunctional families are at the heart of many Bible stories, the origin of its characters, and the destiny of its people. What that has meant to Jewish and Christian writers over the centuries has changed immensely, adapted to the times. This is true of readers today as well. Such adaptations are evident in our current cultural conflicts and how those conflicts reflect, extend, and use biblical stories to new ends.

The chapters of this book will reflect 1) the original themes of the mothers' stories, 2) the long history of their interpretation as they have been told and retold, and 3) how they relate to cultural issues of today, such as,

- deeply ambivalent attitudes towards sexuality, including fear of women's desire,
- the desexualizing, sanitizing, and idealizing of selfless motherhood,
- judgement of women who cannot, or do not choose to, have children,
- secular and religious laws governing reproductive rights such as birth control and abortion, and
- the ignorance, fear, and hostility between races and ethnicities that, as I write in the summer of 2020, have reached crisis proportions in the United States.

All of these appear in abundance in the biblical stories, even if they are spoken of with different words, such as chosen-ness, righteousness, rejected family members, and unacceptable "Others."

These pressing current issues affect everyone today. Therefore, this book is intended for all readers interested in their relationship to biblical stories, readers from any religious, ethical, or nonreligious tradition. I write it with fewer citations than are typically included in scholarly publications. If readers are interested in the texts, theories, background, or rationales that underlie what is offered in the following pages, I invite them to refer to the endnotes I have supplied for that purpose. Restricting such information to endnotes will allow readers who wish to simply read without distracting interruption to do so. In the end, it is the stories that I hope will reverberate within you as you read, stories that are familiar yet distant, painful yet painfully honest. They offer explanations, celebrations, justifications, and condemnations. Stories, however, often reflect the things that we hope for much more than what is the case in our own lives. Let their legacy be better stories, then, and better hopes.

Understanding Motherhood and Peoplehood in Ancient Texts

"Probably there is nothing in human nature more resonant with charges than the flow of energy between two biologically alike bodies, one of which has lain in amniotic bliss inside the other, one of which has labored to give birth to the other. The materials are here for the deepest mutuality and the most painful estrangement."

—Adrienne Rich, *Of Woman Born: Motherhood as Experience and Institution*

Adrienne Rich's groundbreaking *Of Woman Born*, published in 1976, described the ways in which motherhood functions as a cultural institution, that is, as an organizing social structure and a powerfully imposed gender role. Rich argues that the institution of motherhood holds women to impossibly high moral and cultural standards, limiting them to a very constrained set of behaviors, including economic dependence on men. Rich's book explores the long history of motherhood, citing everything from the loss of primal matriarchal societies to the medicalizing of childbirth, such as the replacement of midwives with male doctors. She concludes that motherhood—not in its essence, but as it has been understood culturally—has brought women status, even power, but also constant moral scrutiny and accusation.

Such cultural ideas also run through the stories of the biblical mothers. Through their bodies, they give birth to the chosen people of Israel and the elect Christian church—impressive cultural achievements. Their children are understood as separate and holy peoples, in a special relationship with the divine (God). Their bodies are the means to all of this. Their wombs, breasts, and arms birth, feed, and hold the people of God, according to the Bible. With this has come status and recognition. Biblical mothers have been honored and loved by Jews and Christians over the centuries.

And yet, in their own stories in the Bible they are never presented as the main characters or heroes. They inhabit the worlds of their husbands and sons, Abraham, Isaac, Jacob, David, and Jesus. Their primary (some might say only) importance lies in their ability and potential as carriers of life. So, if their power and status reside in this one ability, why do the biblical stories consistently present them as infertile or virginal, only capable of producing such righteous and blessed sons through miraculous actions of God on their bodies? The mothers of Abraham's family create the nation of Israel in Genesis, but not without divine intervention. Their stories describe God opening and closing their wombs. The very need for this intervention raises questions about whether they are worthy to conceive God's holy people. The Virgin Mary is betrothed, but her marriage has not been consummated and she conceives without having sex, through actions of God's spirit upon her. In Mary's story as well, human sexual reproduction is not enough.

This is a plot twist that is unfortunate because, really, what else did the mothers have going for them? If we look at the Hebrew Bible, we see that wives are described as the property of their husbands, and their primary value is their sexuality and procreative power. Their job is to "build up the house" of their particular patriarch by managing the household and birthing children. As property, they are exchanged between men. They cannot be "stolen"; adultery is punishable by death. Mothers are ideally presented as compassionate, helpful, moral exemplars, and protective defenders of their children. However, the stories also offer variations on these images, such as the barren wife, the foreign wife, and the widow. These women are also mothers, but as aberrations from the ideal they provoke a lot of questions.

In the New Testament, women appear as mothers, prostitutes, poor widows, women with health problems (understood as spiritual disease in the first century), disciples, sisters, and apostles. The two most important women, the Virgin Mary and the disciple Mary Magdalene, embody asexual spirituality and female repentance for past sexual sins, respectively.[1] The underlying duality of virgin-whore that these two women came to symbolize in Christian tradition reflects the dominant worldview in first-century Judea, which split reality into hierarchical opposites defined as good or bad, such as spirit/body, man/woman, celibacy/sexuality, and so on. This was the Neoplatonic philosophical worldview. Such a Greco-Roman frame of reference combined with ancient Jewish ideas about wives, mothers, and other women produced teachings about gender hierarchy within the emerging church. The apostle Paul insisted that women should be obedient to their husbands; he also taught that women should be silent in church, live as moral examples to each other, cover their bodies, and practice celibacy, even, if possible, when married. In a later letter to the church leader Timothy, Paul (or more likely one of his imitators) writes that women are saved, not through their relationship with Christ, but "through motherhood." The regulation of women is not a sidebar in the New Testament.

In later Jewish and Christian writings, questions about the mothers do not go away. Rabbis' and church fathers'[2] discussions of mothers are strewn with worries about the inescapably physical and female procreative process they go through as they produce a chosen nation and an elect church. In these writings, the mothers are conferred power and status, but also provoke suspicion and judgement. So it is that over the centuries the matriarchs have been repeatedly subjected to critical examination of their biological, ethnic, and religious status. Where and who do they come from? Are they faithful and submissive to the God of Abraham, Isaac, and Jacob? Are they virtuous? Is their sexuality untainted by lust, geared only to procreation?

Moving through such commentaries, interpretations, and retellings of the matriarchs' stories, one can sense a good deal of anxiety in the writings of Jewish and Christian authors. If ideal Jewish and Christian religious identity and practice were understood almost entirely in male terms, then what to do with the fact that female bodies and their life-giving power were—and are—needed to produce the ideal men who are believed to be their betters?

This question has caused a lot of cognitive dissonance over time, especially reconciling the power of women's bodies with men's perceived religious righteousness. Charlotte Fonrobert, an expert scholar of rabbinic texts, observes that "the ideal world of the rabbis [and their study of the Bible] is one without women" and this stands in direct contradiction to "the 'real' world of the household, which perpetuates the world of the rabbis via physical reproduction."[3] Similar disconnects are evident in the Christian tradition. Misogyny pervades the writings of influential church fathers, in images of dripping breasts, stinking wombs, and crying babies, as well as exhortations to perpetual virginity. These were men who had taken on a celibate life, foregoing marriage and family to devote themselves to the church and God. Explaining the conception and birthing of Jesus, they had to somehow reconcile their avoidance and fear of sensuality, sexuality, and women's bodies with the fact that Jesus was human, made flesh, born of a woman's body.

Stories about the mothers in the Bible also offer very different descriptions of women, their bodies, and motherhood. For instance, there are quite divergent biblical descriptions of the mothers' conception of their sons.[4] The first human coupling between Adam and Eve is already complicated. Adam has sexual relations with Eve, yet Eve says that she has "created" Cain with God (Genesis 4:1). It seems Eve's reproductive power is fused with God's creative power, more than Adam's. God "opens the wombs" of Sarah, Rebecca, Leah, Rachel, and Ruth, while their human husbands can only pray to God to make their wives conceive. God seems to have exclusive power over these mothers' conceptions.

On the other hand, the laws in the book of Leviticus (called Torah laws) regulate and enforce a woman's virginity and purity to ensure that human fathers are correctly identified. In this case, fathers' defining role in the sexual reproduction of Israel is not only crucial, but also reinforced by law. Could these laws that assure human paternity have served as a counterbalance to the descriptions in the Bible's stories of the reproductive partnership between God and the mothers? It's an interesting question.

Another example that focuses on human and not divine paternity is found in the book of the prophet Jeremiah, where God promises to "sow" Israel and Judah *with the seed of humans*, as the Israelites return home from exile in Babylon. Here, again, the human male "seed" seems crucial and necessary to recreating the chosen people again in their promised land.

As for Mary and her conception of Jesus, God's spirit "comes upon" and "overpowers" her in the Gospel of Luke, while Joseph is pushed emphatically to the sidelines. As we shall see in chapter 4, other early Christian depictions of Mary's conception of Jesus, not found in the New Testament, diverge even further from the Hebrew Bible stories, featuring highly imaginative and unorthodox means of impregnation.

If nothing else, all these examples indicate that conception was a deeply mysterious concept to the ancient Israelites and remained so, still, for first- and second-century Jewish and Christian writers. They also indicate that the power and role of the mothers in conceiving righteous and holy children of God was a continuing question in the biblical authors' minds. The singling out of Israel and the Christian church as chosen, separate, and righteous was tied to how their children were conceived. One thing is clear: mothers alone were not enough to pull it off. So, how do these stories of God-controlled female bodies perfect their imperfection? In order to establish the divine origins of the nation of Israel and of Christian salvation and "the saved," they must do this, but how?

MOTHERHOOD AND PEOPLEHOOD

Ideal versions of motherhood and peoplehood were defined carefully and authoritatively. One powerful method was to contrast the biblical ideals with other imperfect mothers and peoples. Such contrasts are a staple of biblical stories, differentiating the good from the bad. The mothers—indeed most biblical characters—are presented as ideal religious identities or as negative foils that define ideal identities through negative comparison, even if many characters turn out to be much more complex than that. "Good" and "bad" characters are then used to prescribe ideal behaviors in Jewish and Christian communities. For centuries, the rabbinic tradition has drawn inferences from the biblical stories about how to follow Torah law. Likewise, Christian interpretations have used the biblical texts and characters to reinforce and regulate desired religious behaviors in readers of the Bible. Very often it is negative female examples that prop up such behavioral rules and regulations. There have been, however, truly toxic side effects of this method of biblical interpretation.

In the case of the biblical mothers, their role in the (re)production of chosen or elect peoples has continually, for too long, produced brutal understandings of religious "Others," those who are *not* in the family or nation, those *not* saved by Jesus. The visceral claims of family and condemnations of those outside family, tribe, or religious community, are persistent in the Hebrew Bible and the New Testament. They have been reworked and applied in new contexts by leaders of new communities over the centuries. Until very recently, the repeated merging of biological, religious, and moral identity has been a staple of Jewish and Christian traditions. The concept of kinship is a double-edged sword with a range of implications. Being kin can be established through biology, marriage, history, common cause, group consciousness, religion, and, all too often, the rejection and exclusion of "Others." This concept, in the context of the Bible, has allowed, and justified, the idealization or condemnation of entire religious communities. More importantly, it has opened the door for later generations to link biology with group identities, and group identities with moral and physical superiority.

This is evident still today. The merging of motherhood and peoplehood, and the condemning of those not in the "family" or "group" is not merely historical, not only in the past. The way mothers and their procreative power are used to define the favored status of peoples is still very much in play today. The use and regulation of women's wombs in order to produce peoples or nations perceived of as powerful, righteous, and blessed still survives and continues to affect women in our own time. The imposed, involuntary sterilization of black and Native American women in the United States during much of the twentieth century is well-documented.[5] The fight for federally protected reproductive rights, hard-fought and won in Roe v. Wade (1973), has now been lost—at least for now, the right to legal abortions overturned by the Supreme Court of the United States. This has not been a spontaneous reversal, but has been years in the making in America, with the religious right working to vote into power politicians and justices who would ensure the control of women's wombs through legislation. The Catholic Church's opposition and the strong stance of evangelical Protestants on the "right to life" is not a sidebar in this constitutional struggle. *Plus ça change, plus c'est la meme chose*, for such desire to control maternal bodies has been consistently present in the long history of biblical interpretation as well. Whatever one thinks about abortion, the visceral, Christian-aligned political struggle to legislate or liberate women's wombs has a specific, biblically informed history.

Indeed, the sheer volume and variety of laws and stories created to define and constrain women's bodies in exegetical tradition is remarkable. Continual fixation on women's sexuality and procreative power reveals endless concern about maternal bodies in interpretative texts. Assurances and dangers have been continually discussed as Jewish and Christian writers evaluated the biblical practices of incest and endogamy (marriage within the family, tribe, or clan), marrying sister-wives and foreign wives, the "subversive" actions of determined "wannabe" mothers, and the spiritual superiority of virginity and celibacy. The good and bad outcomes of each practice have been judged repeatedly and anxiously in later exegetical writings.

In the Hebrew Bible, the survival of a people and a nation entailed the command to procreate. This command linked holiness and peoplehood to genealogy, women, and wombs. In the New Testament, the survival of Christianity made necessary the cultural appropriation, some would say "theft," of the ancient and respected history and culture of Israel. The God and Scriptures of the Israelite religion were taken and claimed for "the new Israel." The belonging that had been understood as family, tribe, and chosen people was redefined through concepts of spiritual rather than biological (re)birth, accomplished through participation in Jesus' birth, death, and resurrection. This book is a journey through some of the biblical stories that deal with these larger purposes, and how they have been used in some Jewish and Christian writings to authorize the diverse logics of sexual and racial difference we live with today.

Front Matter Endnotes

1. Mary Magdalene is *not* identified as a prostitute in the New Testament. Later Christian writers merged her with other women in the text, including a sinful woman with an alabaster jar who washed Jesus' feet with her tears. In this way, they created a narrative that labeled her as a prostitute. In fact, many scholars believe that Mary Magdalene may have been the first apostle and a close companion of Jesus, the most respected and spiritually advanced of all the disciples. There are several gospel texts that did not make it into the New Testament in which Mary is explicitly named the closest apostle to Jesus and the one with the most knowledge, including *The Gospel of Mary Magdalene.*

2. Rabbinic Judaism, which is the form of Judaism practiced today, began after the Second Temple in Jerusalem was destroyed by the Romans in 70 CE. It grew out of Pharisaic Judaism, which is described in the New Testament (in a one-sided negative way). The rabbis studied Jewish law (Torah) as the Pharisees before them had done. They preserved and expanded upon centuries of Torah commentaries from the second to sixth centuries in collections of those teachings called the Jerusalem and Babylonian Talmuds. The church fathers were authoritative writers in the first centuries of Christianity, leaders in the emerging church who established doctrines, defined religious practices, and denounced any beliefs or practices which differed from their own.

3. When Fonrobert refers to "the world of the rabbis," she refers to male centers of biblical study in which rabbis interpreted and explained Biblical stories and laws, and how their communities should apply them. The Hebrew term for these is *beit midrash. Beit* means "house" and *midrash* is biblical interpretation that explores practical and theological questions, explaining how to follow Jewish law (Torah) and/or elaborating on biblical texts. It often expands stories and laws into sermons, parables, and even folktales. Fonrobert writes about the disconnect between this world and the world of women and mothers in her "Handmaid, the Trickster," 273.

4. Much of what I describe here appears in Stiebert, "Human Conception."

5. Ko, "Unwanted Sterilization," passim. See also Alexandra Minna Stern's award-winning 2015 book *Eugenic Nation.*

I

Birthing the Family of Israel

Mothers and Their Others

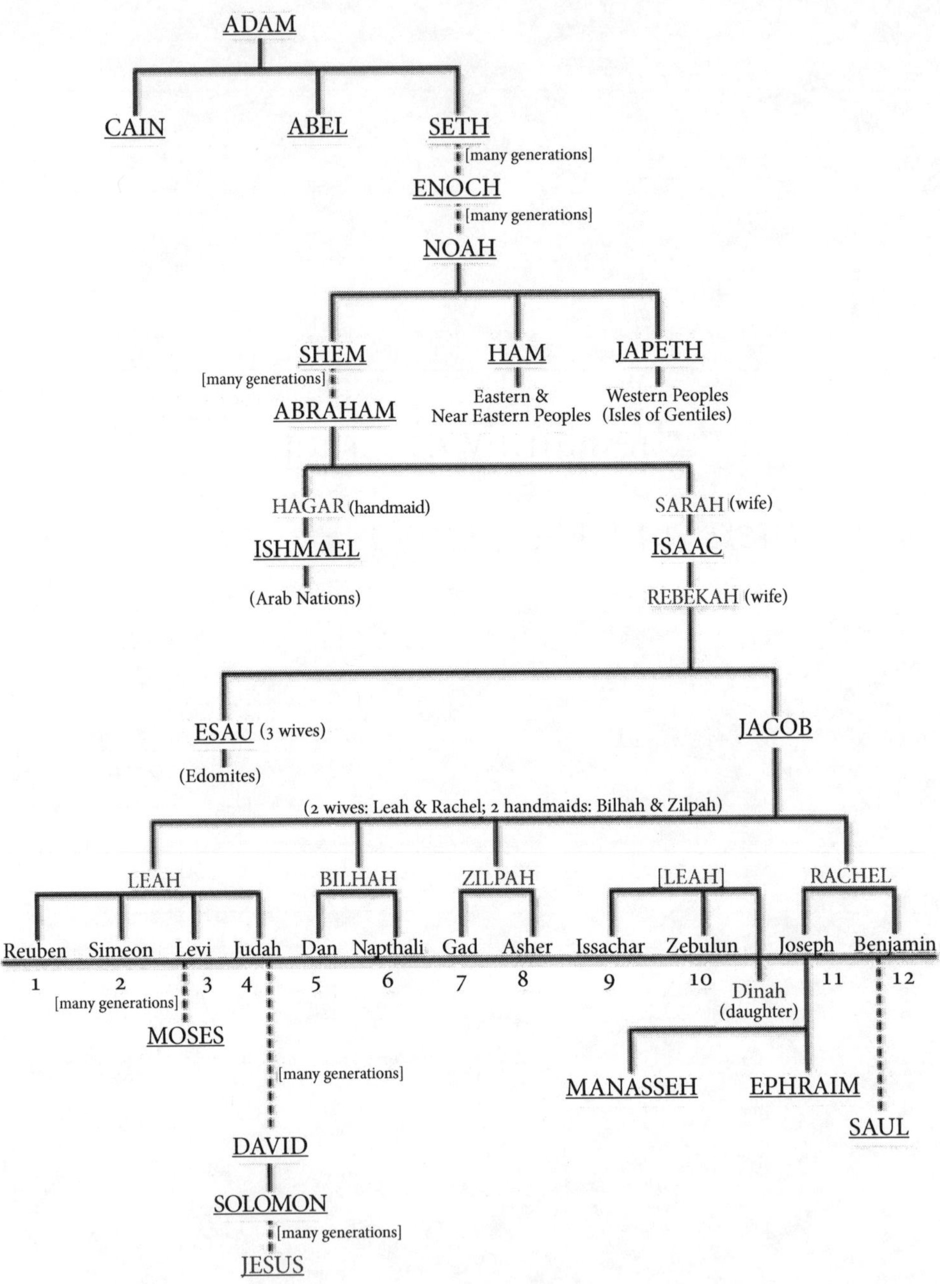

Biblical Genealogy from Adam to Jesus

1

All in the Family: The First Generations

The famous theologian Augustine lived during the fourth century CE. He was bishop of the North African town of Hippo from 395 until his death in 430 and was recognized as a saint shortly after his death. He is one of the most respected leaders of the early church and is responsible for critical doctrinal beliefs that persist today, including the doctrine of original sin, which views all human beings as sinful from birth. His books are filled with praises for chastity, condemnation of sexual desire, and shame in the human body. Of women and sexuality, he wrote the following: "I know nothing which brings the manly mind down from the heights more than a woman's caresses and that joining of bodies without which one cannot have a wife."

Sex, even in marriage, was for Augustine a sin, and when procreation was not possible, as after menopause, it became a major (mortal) sin. He argued that a man should cherish his wife's soul but hate her body as an enemy. He believed that "original sin" was transmitted through sexual reproduction and procreation. This inescapable depraved state of all human beings, tied tightly to sexuality, he laid at the feet of the first mother, specifically, Eve's disobedience in the garden of Eden.[1]

Augustine was writing over a thousand years after some of the stories from the Hebrew Bible that we are looking at, but only three centuries after the New Testament was written. He presented his views on women, wives, mothers, sex, marriage, and salvation as faithful interpretations of what "the Scriptures" had taught. His influence was, and continues to be, definitive in Western Christianity.

Turning to the present, compare the voice of the African American poet Maya Angelou, a consummate poet, whose third volume of poetry,

And Still I Rise, was published in 1978. It is a collection of poems that express a determination to rise above trauma and disadvantage. Angelou has been praised as a writer who captures her culture's written and unwritten heritage, and this is fully evident in the following verses from one of her most famous poems, entitled "Phenomenal Woman." It goes like this:

> Pretty women wonder
> Where my secret lies.
> I'm not cute or built to suit
> A fashion model's size.
> But when I start to tell them,
> They think I'm telling lies.
> I say,
> It's in the reach of my arms,
> The span of my hips,
> The stride of my step,
> The curl of my lips.
> I'm a woman phenomenally.
> Phenomenal woman, that's me.
>
> I walk into a room
> Just as cool as you please,
> And to a man,
> The fellows stand or
> Fall down on their knees.
> Then they swarm around me,
> A hive of honeybees.
> I say,
> It's the fire in my eyes,
> And the flash of my teeth,
> The swing in my waist,
> And the joy in my feet.
> I'm a woman phenomenally.
> Phenomenal woman, that's me.
>
> Men themselves have wondered
> What they see in me.
> They try so much
> But they can't touch
> My inner mystery.
> When I try to show them,
> They say they still can't see.
> I say,

It's in the arch of my back,
The sun of my smile,
The ride of my breasts,
The grace of my style.
I'm a woman phenomenally.
Phenomenal woman, that's me.

Now you understand
Just why my head's not bowed.
I don't shout or jump about
Or have to talk real loud.
When you see me passing,
It ought to make you proud.
I say,
It's in the click of my heels,
The bend of my hair,
the palm of my hand,
The need for my care.
'Cause I'm a woman phenomenally.
Phenomenal woman, that's me.

I juxtapose these two visions here, of women, their bodies, and the pleasure they are capable of feeling and inspiring, to create a conversation between the dominant early church fear and rejection of women, sex, and desire and the need today for women to exorcise such attitudes from their own self-image. That need is only made more urgent by more recent cultural messaging, such as the devaluation of black beauty by white culture or myths about black women's sexuality.

This toxic combination of racism and sexism finds ancient parallels in the biblical stories, but with some historical qualifications. The concept we call "race" was created in the nineteenth century as a set of beliefs about the genetic superiority of certain groups over others in the human population. It was propagated in England by Charles Darwin's cousin, Francis Galton, and was applied in America first through laws prohibiting interracial marriage. In the ancient Near East and during the first centuries of Christianity, the concept of "race" did not exist. Instead, the Hebrew Bible and New Testament speak of "nations" or "peoples," terms that are closely related conceptually to our word "ethnicity." These words referred to the shared origins, history, religion, culture, and destiny of peoples. In the New Testament, it also often refers to non-Jewish peoples. Nonetheless, these terms do often share a logic of negative contrast. In the biblical texts, there are explicit and repeated passages that focus on relative beauty, and dangerous or suspicious "foreign" status and undesirability. A good example can be found in early Jewish condemnations of Canaanite women's insatiable lust, as we shall see in the coming pages.

The contrast between Augustine and Angelou thus provides a useful frame for considering the stories about the biblical mothers and their role in the creation of chosen people. The biblical stories are also focused on the worth of female bodies and male hyper-vigilance of them. The mothers are also subjected to sexual, moral, and ethnic judgement. Could they really embody the deep relationship between the Israelites and God? Could they really partake in the mutual promise—the covenant—of love and righteousness that God shares with their sons? The biblical authors tied these questions to doubts about the moral and physical righteousness of the mothers. Perhaps this is why, more than once, God's intervention is needed to create Israel, opening and closing the mothers' wombs. Neither the mothers—nor the fathers for that matter—seem to be able to (pro)create Israel alone.

Yet, the solution of God intervening, opening and closing the mothers' wombs did not put an end to questions about the mothers. Over and over again, in the book of Genesis, drama and anxiety erupt in worries about wives becoming mothers. Barren wives pray, meddle, and hatch plans in order to have sons. Foreign wives enter the family, yet are seen as religiously, morally, or sexually dangerous. Children fall outside the promise and leave the family, giving birth to other peoples. All these situations call into question the idea of a family and a people set apart by God as holy.

The question that will not go away in Genesis seems simple at first: "Who is family and who is not-family, or 'Other'?" This question essentially asks who is right with God: Who is religiously righteous and who is not? Because of this, the stories about the mothers end up establishing religious and moral boundaries between peoples or nations, as they tell the story of the birth of Israel. The character of groups, including Israelites, are explained through their birth origins. Being in the family is about the circumstances of one's birth, but also religious and social practices of righteousness, based in the covenant with God. Children stand for the transmission of that covenant and those practices across generations. Israel's chosenness and difference from other peoples are created through family origins and birth histories.

Even with all of that in place, however, there is yet another twist. This birth-embedded differentiation process between good and bad peoples gets more complicated in the mothers' stories because the origins of Israel and the peoples closest to Israel turn out to be intimately bound together, from the beginning. These "peoples," embodied in the mothers and their children, move in and out of *the same family*. Sarah and her slave, Hagar; Lot's daughters; Rebecca; Leah and Rachel and their slaves, Zilpah and Bilhah; Tamar, who is a Canaanite; and Ruth, who is Moabite: they are all central to the story of Israel. They are thus all "family," even as they come from different places and cultures. Slaves, wives, sisters, daughters, and daughters-in-law embody a range of social and cultural identities. And their children become Israel and the nations around it. Divisions in the family and divisions in the nation, not unlike the history of divisions in our own time.

It is worth reflecting for a moment on the complexity of these relationships of deep familial bonds, betrayal, and division. Even as the stories about the mothers try to establish the family of Israel and its unique relationship to God, they end up blurring lines of difference between Israel and surrounding peoples. Abraham has a son with an Egyptian slave woman, Hagar. Their son creates, with his own Egyptian wife, a neighboring people, the Ishmaelites. Lot's daughters give birth to enemy nations, the Moabites and Ammonites, whom they conceive with their father (Abraham's nephew). Isaac and Rebecca's twins, Jacob and Esau, compete with each other to be the next Abrahamic patriarch, and when Jacob wins, Esau leaves, marries outside the family, as Ishmael had before him, and becomes the father of yet another nation, the Edomites. Judah and his daughter-in-law, Tamar the Canaanite, give birth to twins, Perez and Zerah, only to have Perez become the forefather of the Jewish-Christian messiah, Jesus. Who is "family"? Who is Israel and who are Christians when birth origins are so intertwined?

The mothers are at the heart of these questions, as are the specific details of the conception and birthing of their children. Understanding their role will mean paying attention to the kinds of sexual, reproductive, and ethical strategies that are offered in their stories to establish clear boundaries between peoples. That those strategies have been interpreted and judged by later Jewish and Christian writers makes clear that establishing Israel's and Christianity's identities did not end with the stories of the Bible. It continued to be explored and explained in ever-changing times and places. The strategies put forward in these stories may seem unbelievable or even unacceptable, depending upon who is hearing them and when, including you and me. Then again, they may seem all too familiar.

SEX IN THE FAMILY: INCEST, SISTER-WIVES, AND "ETHNIC" WIVES

From the beginning, the Hebrew Bible describes the peoples of the world and how they relate to each other as family. Adam and Eve are the father and mother of humankind.[2] Adam has also been understood by some as the father of Eve, since she is created out of his body. Noah's three sons generate all the families on earth. This theme of procreating and marrying within the same family (incest) also recurs in the mothers' stories. This often provokes uncomfortable questions in readers today, especially since these stories evaluate the practice of incest positively, at least some of the time. Incest is seen as essential to producing righteous Israel not only in the Bible itself, but in later interpretations of its stories. It appears in Israel's family line for many generations. Abraham and his half-sister Sarah marry in Mesopotamia. Isaac weds Rebekah, his cousin. Leah and Rachel are Jacob's cousins, and they are also sisters. Judah marries his daughter-in-law, Tamar. Thus, daughters-in-law, half-sisters, and cousins consistently produce offspring in the line from Adam to Israel's twelve tribes and beyond.

This list of beloved patriarchs and matriarchs can only mean that in the Hebrew Bible incest is understood as good, at least in these cases. It is seen as producing spiritual righteousness and holiness. This is a difficult read for many today. It is true that incest is also sometimes seen as negative in the stories, but the very openness to any possible value in incest is hard for many to absorb, even when historical context is accounted for. It is hard to write about as well, knowing that incest causes such deep suffering in our own time. Incest is present in all social classes, in developed as well as developing countries. The World Health Organization has classified incest as a silent health emergency. Father-daughter incest is reported to be the most common type, followed by other types like brother-sister, sister-sister, and mother-son incest. It is interesting that mother-daughter incest is virtually invisible in common data sets today, as it is in the biblical stories, yet it also exists today.[3] Speaking from my own experience, too many of my women friends have suffered the reality of incest. The fact that incest is an experience shared and sometimes valued in biblical stories and interpretations of them across the centuries, and that this could cause confusion, pain, even acceptance of it, is distressing.

At the same time, incest is present in the creation myths and folklore of most cultures and the taboo against the practice is also virtually universal. The Hebrew Bible did not invent such stories. In fact, father-daughter incest is relatively rare in the Hebrew Bible as a whole. The laws of Leviticus 18 and 20 set clear boundaries, condemning incestuous relations in the family. Although Leviticus is less clear in forbidding father-daughter relations, there is clear concern about incest in the culture. Hebrew Bible scholar Johanna Stiebert does excellent, insightful research on gender, family relations, and the Bible. She writes that the scarcity of father-daughter incest stories in the Hebrew Bible, as well as the general incest laws "seem to reflect a wider, near-universal abhorrence of incest, especially first-degree sexual encounter."[4]

It is certainly helpful to contextualize stories of incest in this way, yet readers do not always have access to such data and their responses will inevitably vary. The stories are still painful to many when they make connections between elements in the stories and the situation for many women today. Below, I will discuss what problems the authors seem to be trying to solve, what hopes they express in their stories, and what worries weigh them down. Their depiction of sexual practices serves to establish Israel as a family set apart by God and sex in the family was linked to this larger agenda. Yet, from another vantage point, these stories also appear to be working through and questioning many of the practices and values they depict. On this level, the authors seem to be examining the ideals they have inherited.

The need to explain Israel's chosenness is expressed at least partly through stories of incest. This is why it is sometimes presented as a good way to preserve Israel's holy seed and to ensure the continuation of God's chosen people. Furthermore, this is not an ancient strategy that only exists in the earliest stories. In later Jewish retellings of the stories, examples of incest are actually *added in*.

A good example of this is *Jubilees*, a second-century-BCE rewriting of the Hebrew Bible stories. This book adds many story elements that are not in the Bible as we have it today. Why would the author add instances of incest into the stories of Israel's founding? Well, one thing we know about the author is that he was very concerned about his Jewish audience remaining separate and independent from the Greek culture that had become dominant in Palestine at the time he was writing (centuries after Genesis began to be written down). This was a time when the Judeans (the name of the Israelites at that time) had been conquered by the Greeks, their land occupied, and their culture dominated by new, Greek ideas and social structures. The question of how Judean religion and culture would survive was real. Many Judeans embraced the new culture and found ways to combine their own traditions with it, but many were worried about losing their identity and religion.

The author of *Jubilees* belonged to the latter group, so it makes sense that the biblical themes of incest and marrying within the family are expanded in his book. Adam and Eve's sons engage in incest, an addition that does not appear in Genesis. Not only is this necessary according to the logic of the story—there's no one else on earth, after all—it is also a most effective way of having the first primal ancestors model incest. Cain produces a son with Awan, his full sister, as does his brother Seth with his full sister Azura. Adam and Eve's other children take sisters and nieces for their wives. This continues through to Noah, who also takes a niece as his wife. These unions do not appear in the Hebrew Bible, but—and this is important—they do get reproduced in later rabbinic writings. In such retellings and repetitions, questions and answers about Israel's separate and holy identity continue to be linked to the practice of incest, long after the biblical stories were originally created.

What is particularly striking about the *Jubilees* version of these stories is that, *in the Bible stories themselves,* the ideals of incest and marrying within the family are *not* presented so straightforwardly. Instead, complications and questions continually surface around these practices. The mothers are carefully evaluated according to their status as family or not-family, as sisters, daughters(-in-law), foreign, or stranger wives. Even sister-wives, who have good family credentials, are continually scrutinized regarding their status as seed-bearers. Their place in the family is repeatedly questioned, as are their religious obedience and potential for "strangeness." They were, after all, critical to the production of Israel's moral and religious purity, relative to surrounding peoples.

Yet, if incest is generally preferred in these stories, the story in Genesis of the first matriarch, Sarah, and her slave, Hagar, puts that preference to the test. Both bore sons to the first patriarch, Abraham, one a sister, one an "outsider." The central contrast between Sarah and Hagar is nothing less than a question posed. If insider status as sister-wives were generally presented as added insurance that the mothers of Israel would transmit the righteousness of Abraham to his offspring, why then is the story of Sarah and Hagar so conflict-ridden? And why is Hagar, an Egyptian slave, an ethnic "Other," clearly perceived as "foreign" and potentially dangerous, included at all? In Sarah and Hagar's story the conflict is between a sister-wife and a foreign wife, yet it does not go predictably. Sarah is not always seen as good, and Hagar is protected and blessed by God. Just how do Sarah and Hagar measure up to the task of creating a chosen people?

THE JOURNEYS OF SARAH AND HAGAR: BARREN AND DESPERATE MOTHERS

The comparative worth of sister-wives and foreign wives is a central question in the story of Abraham, Sarah, and Hagar. Their story can be found in chapters 12, 15–18, and 20–21 of the book of Genesis. Over the course of those chapters, Sarah's status as Abraham's sister changes as does Hagar's status as an unimportant, expendable Egyptian slave. These changes in their statuses also define the worthiness of their children. Which mother is good enough to birth the promised child of the covenant, the one whom God would bless with abundance, many children, land, power, and nations? In a very real sense, God's promise is up for grabs. Is Sarah or Hagar the mother of the promise?

In Genesis 16, we learn that Sarah is barren. Her status is shaky. Before that, in Genesis 11:31 she is first described as the daughter-in-law of Terah (Abraham's father) and Abraham's wife, not even a sister-wife. Then, in Genesis 12, when she and Abraham travel to Egypt, Abraham asks her to tell the Egyptians that she is his sister. He apparently fears they will kill him if she is thought to be his wife: because of her beauty, he believes they would want to give her to Pharaoh. All this is made clear in Genesis 12:11–13, which reads as follows:

> When he was about to enter Egypt, he said to his wife Sarah, "I know well that you are a woman beautiful in appearance; and when the Egyptians see you, they will say, 'This is his wife,' then they will kill me, but they will let you live. Say you are my sister, so that it may go well with me because of you, and that my life may be spared on your account."

The goal is to preserve Abraham's life in a foreign land, even if it means Sarah being taken as a concubine by Pharaoh. That this is a lie and that she is not his sister is clear. However, later in Genesis 20:12, when Abraham repeats this strategy, this time in the territory of a king named Abimelech, Abraham describes Sarah as his half sister, "the daughter of my father, but not the daughter of my mother."

The shifts in Sarah's status in these episodes are important. They force attention to her standing. She is and is not his sister. Her sexual purity is put in question. She is made sexually available to other men by her husband, yet the biblical authors are quick to offer assurances that God keeps her from actually being touched when in the custody of the "foreign" men. Her sexual and family status is repeatedly endangered and then rescued. In the end, her transformation into a sister moves her progressively from barren, potentially strange, outsider wife to ideal in-family motherhood. It just takes time. In contrast, Hagar always remains definitively outside the family, an Egyptian and a slave. Both women, then, have uncertain worth, but Sarah emerges as the insider protected by God, if not by her husband.

Sarah becomes a sister-wife, then, but the exploration of her worth does not end there. She is still depicted as making some troubling choices. Remember, in Genesis 16, Sarah is presented as infertile and anxious. As a result, she encourages Abraham to take her Egyptian slave Hagar as a surrogate mother. By the legal customs of that time, the child would be Sarah's.

As we will discover moving through the mothers' stories, this is the first of many bed-tricks that the mothers arrange to meet their maternal obligations. In the case of Sarah's bed-trick, Abraham is aware of the arrangement and the plan falls within Israelite law.

Sarah's scheme, however, becomes increasingly problematic as the story continues. It causes more difficulties than it solves. In later writings (to be discussed below), it is even depicted as religiously disobedient and dangerous. In those later accounts, Sarah is portrayed as improperly taking the life-giving reproductive power of God into her own hands. Remember that the Hebrew Bible God is a God of the womb, who opens and closes wombs as he creates his chosen people. Who is this woman to intervene in his divine plan and power, to humanly engineer the child of God's promise? As Abraham's sister, Sarah may have satisfied the preference for in-family unions, but as rogue manipulator of the family seed, she appears disobedient, a stranger-within.

In the end, Sarah's strategy fails, leaving her regretting the status that Hagar's son, Ishmael, has acquired, as well as the power the birth has conferred onto Hagar. So, Sarah rejects her legal connection to her half-Egyptian son, Ishmael, and exiles him and his mother, Hagar, into the desert. God tells Abraham to go along with the plan; that he should listen to his wife.

Now, one would think, given the positive depictions of in-family lineage, incest, and procreation that Hagar, the outsider, the slave, the one exiled from the family by Sarah and Abraham in Genesis 21, would be expelled without comment or concern. Good riddance to her child as well, the "wrongly" conceived, humanly engineered child of the outsider mother. But it is not so. In Genesis 21, God saves Hagar and her son Ishmael from certain death in the desert, supplying a well with water to quench their thirst. He hears Ishmael crying and promises to make a great nation out of him too. He stays with the boy as he grows up in the wilderness. After that, Hagar arranges for him to marry an Egyptian woman, like herself.

Why is this addendum that recounts the fate of Hagar and Ishmael included in the book of Genesis? Historically minded readers might point out that it helpfully explains the origins of the Ishmaelites, a neighboring people to the south. However, explaining their origins could have been achieved without suggesting that the Hebrew God was instrumental in protecting and blessing the Ishmaelites. If Hagar's story is about differentiating between Israel and other peoples, however, then the rescue in the desert has a strong message. It argues that paternal seed, lineage, and inheritance are also important in God's interventions. Ishmael is proof of the faithfulness of God's promises to Abraham. He is from Abraham's seed, one of the many nations Abraham was promised by God. Ishmael may not be *the* child of the promise, according to the Hebrew Bible narrative, yet he is a son of Abraham.

In the end, however, all that becomes a secondary concern. Sarah is defined as the mother of God's promise in contrast to Hagar, the Egyptian, who is indisputably an "Other," just as Hagar's son, Ishmael, is transformed from family to "Other" by Sarah. The claim of Sarah and Isaac to unequivocal kinship status is solidified through the greater "otherness" of Hagar and Ishmael.

MORE BARRENNESS AND BED-TRICKS: CONCEIVING AT ALL COSTS

There are three generations from Abraham and Sarah to the twelve tribes of Israel; that is three generations of mothers who conceive Israel. If in the first generation Sarah hatched a scheme, using Hagar as her pawn, in the second generation her son Isaac's wife, Rebecca, is also a schemer.

The story of Isaac, Rebecca, and their twin sons Jacob and Esau can be found in Genesis 25:19–32 and 26:34–28:9. Their story, like Abraham and Sarah's, is filled with concerns about conception, birthing, inheritance, and foreign wives. It begins with Rebecca's inability to have a child and ends with her son Esau marrying his exiled uncle Ishmael's daughter.

Like Sarah, Rebecca is a barren wife and must depend on God to open her womb. Her husband Isaac can only pray that God might make her conceive. When she does, it is with twin boys (Jacob and Esau) who, God tells her, are warring nations in her womb. Indeed, Esau is born first, yet Jacob immediately follows, grasping the heel of his brother's foot to pull him back and gain the firstborn position. We might be forgiven for thinking this is probably not what she wished for: her very womb becomes a battleground in the male struggle to be chosen as God's favored seed. Yet Rebecca endures, has her twin boys, and becomes determined that her second son should be chosen as the next family patriarch. She devises a trick to ensure her younger son, Jacob, will inherit the promises given to Abraham and Isaac. She has Jacob pretend to be Esau on Isaac's deathbed so that he can get Isaac's last and binding blessing. This inheritance rightfully belonged to her firstborn Esau, and undoing that birthright is transgressive to say the least. The father is tricked; the mother prevails. Yet another bed-trick, though this time not sexual in nature.

Once again, a mother's story provokes questions about whether her actions are virtuous. Once again, no simple answers are given. For instance, in Genesis 27:11–13, while hatching her plan with Jacob, Rebecca offers to take the blame for their actions:

> But Jacob said to his mother Rebekah, "Look, my brother Esau is a hairy man, and I am a man of smooth skin. Perhaps my father will feel me, and I shall seem to be mocking him, and bring a curse on myself and not a blessing." His mother said to him, "Let your curse be on me, my son; only obey my word."

Here Rebecca acknowledges not only the unjust nature of their actions; she knows what she is doing is culturally wrong. Isaac also denounces the deception once Esau returns and all becomes clear, though Isaac's anger is directed towards Jacob and not Rebecca. He too acknowledges the sinfulness of the trick as he laments with Esau, "Your brother came deceitfully, and he has taken away your blessing." Finally, when Esau plans to kill Jacob in retaliation, Rebecca insists Jacob go and live with her brother Laban in Haran until Esau's "fury turns away." Would Jacob need to flee if he was in the right? All these developments seem to condemn Rebecca's bed-trick. And yet, the story also shows that she succeeds in shaping the lineage of Israel. Jacob has the blessing of Isaac, even after the sorry truth is brought to light. This would seem to vindicate her actions, especially as Jacob becomes more and more heroic in later passages.

Is there something about Rebecca that allows her to escape questioning and judgement? Perhaps her scheming is balanced out by her insider status in the family, not as sister, in this case, but as Isaac's first cousin. If she flouts the law of primogeniture, she is still one of God's chosen. This is certainly not lost on later writers. It should not be surprising that the author of *Jubilees,* who was so concerned about preserving Israel intact and separate from Greek culture, holds Rebecca up as an ideal of purity of ancestry, as Isaac's first cousin. By the second century, when *Jubilees* is written, she has become the consummate insider.

For example, even Rebecca's trickery is vindicated through the addition of several plot twists in *Jubilees*. First, in the *Jubilees* version, it is Abraham, even before Rebecca, who favors Jacob over Esau. Abraham identifies Jacob as the inheritor of the promise, telling Rebecca, "I know that the LORD will choose him for himself as a people who will rise up from all the nations which are upon the earth." This move to raise up the second son is not the work of the mother after all, but of God himself. Rebecca may look transgressive, but she is in fact bringing God's plan to fruition. The matrix of family, mother, and God is the engine that brings about the destiny of Israel, and it must be maintained and preserved. Thus, in *Jubilees* 22:20–22, as Jacob flees to Haran, Abraham warns him,

> Be careful, my son, Jacob, that you do not take a wife from any of the seed of the daughters of Canaan, because all of his [Canaan's] seed is (destined) for uprooting from the earth; because through the sin of Ham, Canaan sinned,[5] and all of his seed will be blotted out from the earth, and all his remnant. . . . [F]or all of those who worship idols and for the hated ones, there is no hope in the land of the living.

In Genesis, it is Isaac and not Abraham who issues this warning to Jacob, yet here *Jubilees* strengthens the command by making it come from Abraham.

As if that were not enough, *Jubilees* also has Rebecca repeat the warning in language that specifically denounces Canaanite women. No such warning from Rebecca appears in Genesis. She only complains to Isaac that if Jacob marries a foreign wife, her life will be no good to her. Compare the *Jubilees* version of Rebecca's speech (*Jubilees* 25:1–3):

> My son, do not take for yourself a wife from the daughters of Canaan as did Esau your brother, who took for himself two wives from the daughters of Canaan. And they have embittered my soul with all their impure deeds because all their deeds are fornication and lust. And there is not any righteousness with them because their deeds are evil . . . You will take for yourself a wife from my father's house. And the Most High God will bless you, and your children will be a righteous generation and a holy seed.

When Jacob swears, in response, to marry within the family, Rebecca praises God for giving her "a pure son and a holy seed" and in *Jubilees* 25:12–13 speaks to Jacob in the procreative language of her own body:

> The womb of the one who bore you likewise blesses you. My affection and my breasts are blessing you; and my mouth and tongue are praising you greatly. Increase and overflow in the land, and may your seed be perfected in every age in the joy of heaven and earth.

It is fascinating that in an exchange so concerned with the fathers' *seed,* Rebecca's body is described so vividly, specifically as having the power to bless, while Canaanite women's bodies are depicted as sinful, destructive, and dangerous. The right maternal body must be chosen and is essential to "perfecting" God's holy seed. This seems to be more important even than a mother's obedience or righteousness.

How, then, does this emphasis on marriage within the family play out in the third generation? To begin with, Jacob does indeed travel to Haran, lives with and works for his uncle Laban (his mother's brother), and marries his cousins, Leah and Rachel. Leah and Rachel are sisters and they too become Abrahamic mothers, giving birth (along with their slaves Zilpah and Bilhah) to twelve sons, whose descendants become the twelve tribes of Israel. It is a foundational story of great significance in the history of Israel. However, none of this happens without a good deal of desperation, determination, and trickery on Leah's and Rachel's parts, including their use of their slaves, as Sarah before them had done, to conceive sons.

Tensions begin when Jacob is forced by his uncle, Laban, to marry Leah first, though he is in love with, and has asked to marry, Rachel. This is accomplished through yet another bed-trick. Jacob thinks he's marrying Rachel, but in fact marries Leah. Laban sends Leah into his tent and Jacob is unaware of the switch until the morning. Seven years later, Jacob finally marries Rachel. Predictably, however, it soon becomes clear that she, like the mothers before her, is barren. Rachel watches, desolated, as her sister, Leah, bears Jacob son after son. Like Sarah, she gives her slave to her husband when she cannot conceive on her own. She pleads with Jacob, "Give me children or I shall die!" but Jacob's reply once again makes clear who is in control of the mothers' wombs: "Am I in the place of God, who has withheld from you the fruit of the womb?"

More bed-tricks seem inevitable, given the mothers' plight. Next, Leah stops conceiving and is distraught. She sends her slave to Jacob to bear more sons, which is successful for a time. Then one day Leah's son Reuben brings her mandrakes, a plant believed to be an aphrodisiac that boosts fertility. Rachel, who has not yet conceived a son on her own, realizes Leah's plan to conceive again and quickly interrupts it, asking her to give the mandrakes to her instead. Leah refuses. Thus, the competition between Sarah and Hagar is repeated in this story, now between sisters within the chosen family. As the favored wife, however, Rachel controls who Jacob sleeps with. She barters with Leah to give the mandrakes to her in exchange for a night with Jacob, whom Leah loves. Both go on to conceive sons, but the story makes clear that it is God who hears their prayers and opens their wombs.

All these Abrahamic mothers—sisters, cousins, slaves, Israelite and foreign, despairing, determined, powerful—must conceive children or die, as Rebecca says. Their actions are not always culturally acceptable, yet Genesis does not judge them simplistically. Rather, the stories keep open religious and ethical questions about them, their plights, and their chosen sons. The criteria for judgement of the mothers shift often. Later Jewish and Christian writings, however, draw more decisive conclusions about their spiritual knowledge and obedience, as we shall see in Part II, but there is little consensus in them. The open-ended quality of the biblical stories makes that difficult. These first mothers meant so many things to the sons of Israel and who they wished to be. However, before we look at interpretations of the mothers' stories across the centuries, we need to move on to the Davidic mothers, Lot's daughters, Rahab, Tamar, and Ruth. These are the mothers who ensured the birth of King David, the continuation of his seed, and the birth of the Christian messiah, Jesus. Their stories contain many of the same questions, but intensified, as they explain the maternal origins of the golden age and greatest king of Israel.

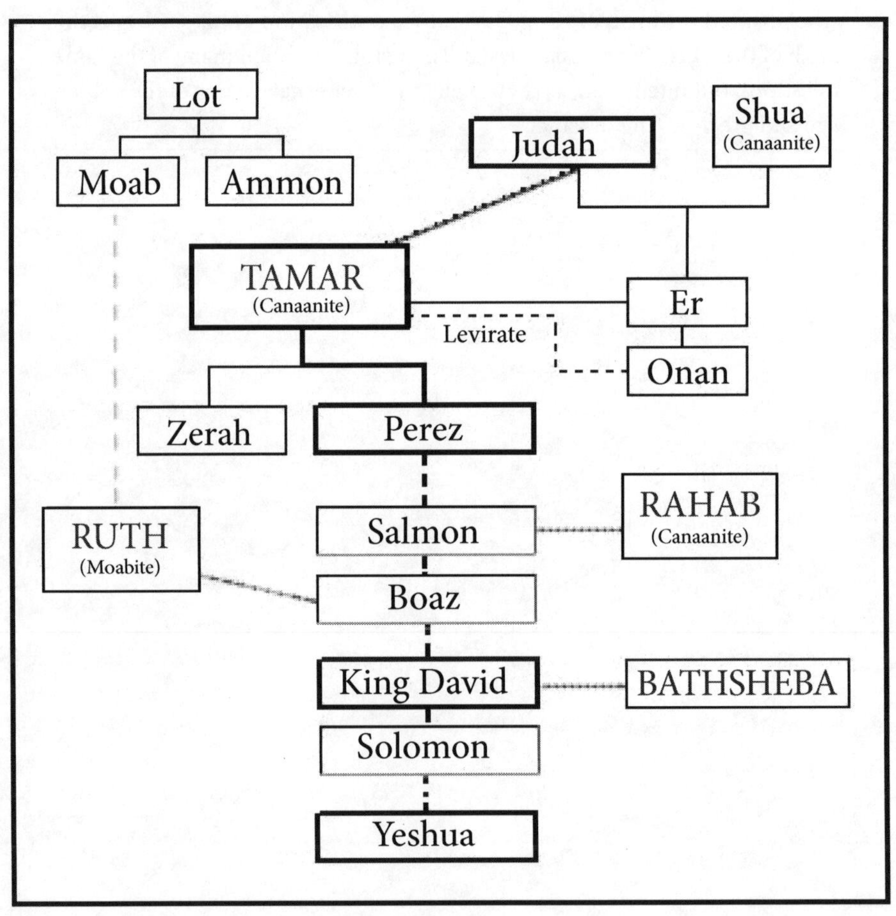
Lot
Moab
Ammon
Judah
Shua
(Canaanite)
TAMAR
(Canaanite)
Er
Levirate
Onan
Zerah
Perez
Salmon
RAHAB
(Canaanite)
RUTH
(Moabite)
Boaz
King David
BATHSHEBA
Solomon
Yeshua

2

Birthing the King: Mothers with Moxie

As you may recall, "the Davidic mothers" are the foremothers of the Israelite king, David. They include Lot's daughters, Rahab the prostitute, Tamar the Canaanite, and Ruth the Moabite. One way to immediately understand their place in Israelite and Christian history is to look at two key Bible passages, the first chapter of the Gospel of Matthew and two verses from the book of Ruth. Both emphasize that the Davidic mothers are linked to, and yet different from, the matriarchs of Genesis.

In the first chapter of Matthew's Gospel, the author offers a genealogy of Jesus of Nazareth, the Christian messiah, in which he biologically links Jesus to the patriarchs of Genesis, the Davidic mothers, and Israel's united monarchy under King David. Such a lineage makes big claims about Jesus' special status in the eyes of the author and his audience, namely that he is the promised future Davidic king of Israel. Here are the relevant verses from Matthew 1:1–16, which link Jesus to the Hebrew Bible patriarchs and matriarchs. I have bolded key phrases.

> An account of the genealogy of Jesus the Messiah, the son of David, **the son of Abraham**. Abraham was the father of **Isaac**, and Isaac the father of Jacob, and **Jacob** the father of **Judah** and his brothers, and **Judah the father of Perez and Zerah by Tamar** . . . and Salmon the father of Boaz by **Rahab**, and **Boaz the father of Obed by Ruth**, and Obed the father of Jesse, and **Jesse the father of King David**. And David was the father of Solomon by the wife of Uriah. . . . and **Jacob the father of Joseph the husband of Mary**, of whom **Jesus** was born, who is called the Messiah.

The mothers in this genealogy are understood as key to the birth of the great Israelite king, David, and of Jesus, the Christian messiah. (Actually, both David and Jesus bore the title of "messiah," or *mashiach*, a Hebrew word which simply meant that they were anointed by God to protect, lead, and save the chosen people of God. It is only later in Christianity that the title "messiah" comes to mean "unique" and "divine." In Jewish tradition, there are many messiahs, many kings, many priests, anointed by God to protect, lead, and save God's people.)

In any case, the mothers in Matthew's genealogy birth the messiahs of their people. You might expect them to be paragons of virtue, and yet, they are not, at least not by the traditional standards of their time. In fact, by those standards, all of them, except Mary, commit sexually aggressive, immodest, and devious acts, engaging in sexual subterfuge, tricking men in order to become mothers. In addition, Rahab, Tamar, and Ruth are not Israelites; they are foreign women, which you may recall from the stories we've seen so far would not have been considered ideal. Yet, according to their stories, they bear the holy men who bring into being the golden age of Israelite history and the salvation of humanity.

Like Matthew's genealogy, but written centuries before Matthew's Gospel, are two verses in the book of Ruth. They also link the Davidic mothers to the Abrahamic matriarchs, establishing their shared role in creating and preserving Israel. Ruth 4:11–12 comes at the end of the story of Ruth, a young widow from Moab who travels back to Bethlehem with her mother-in-law, Naomi, after her husband dies. Indeed, they are both widows with no means of support. Naomi and her husband, who are originally from Bethlehem, travel to Moab during a famine, and Naomi's husband dies there. Ruth marries Naomi's son, who then also dies. When Naomi and Ruth get back to Bethlehem, an older man named Boaz, who is a relative of her late husband, allows them to take food from his fields and eventually marries Ruth. The verses here are a blessing that the people of Bethlehem pray at the marriage of Ruth and Boaz.

> Then all the people who were at the gate, along with the elders, said, "We are witnesses. May the Lord make the woman who is coming into your [Boaz's] house like Rachel and Leah, who together built up the house of Israel. May you produce children in Ephrathah and bestow a name in Bethlehem; and, through the children that the LORD will give you by this young woman, may your house be like the house of Perez, whom Tamar bore to Judah.

This passage is immediately followed by a genealogy of King David, which makes clear (just as Matthew's genealogy above does) that Ruth's child, Obed, was the grandfather of King David himself. Like Rachel, Leah, and Tamar, she is instrumental in the building up of Israel through her childbearing.

Now, parts of the story of how Ruth, a "foreign" and destitute widow, managed to marry Boaz, a wealthy Israelite, are a little less lofty in tone than this marriage blessing. In fact, some might say Ruth's story is sexy and scandalous. However, we are getting ahead of ourselves. We should start with the story of Lot's daughters, the first of the Davidic mothers, especially since one of them is Ruth's foremother.

THE STORY OF LOT'S DAUGHTERS

The story of Lot's daughters is difficult to absorb for many readers today, undoubtedly because it features sex between Abraham's nephew, Lot, and his daughters. It is told in its entirety in Genesis 19, sandwiched between, and then at the end of, the story of God's destruction of the city of Sodom. Yet, even though what happens to the daughters is disturbing to readers today and may be to you as you read through this section, the daughters are not without power or agency. Like the Davidic mothers who follow them, they take matters into their own hands to preserve the family line. Their story is important to our exploration of the mothers who birth Israel because theirs is the story of how God saves Lot and preserves his (Abrahamic) "seed," as well as how King David comes to be.

The story of Lot's daughters is full of twists and turns. For instance, they give birth to enemy nations, the Moabites and the Ammonites, yet out of the Moabites Ruth arises, foremother of King David and Jesus. Out of the Ammonites comes Naamah, the wife of David's grandson, Rehoboam, who, as his wife, also continues the Davidic lineage. It's clear that while Lot's daughters and the conception and birth of their children may give rise to enemy nations, those children are also crucial to the future of the nation of Israel, as well as the birth of the "new Israel," Christianity, in the person of Jesus.

The story goes that angels of God rescue Lot, his wife, and his daughters before God destroys the sinful city of Sodom, all because Lot is Abraham's nephew. Lot's Sodomite wife disobeys the angels' command not to look back as the city is destroyed and is immediately turned into a pillar of salt. So much for the foreign wife in this story . . .

After the destruction of Sodom and the land around it, Lot and his daughters take shelter in a cave in the mountains outside Zoar, a small city in the Jordan Valley that had escaped destruction. The daughters seem to think they are the only human beings left on earth, along with their father. The older says to the younger, "Our father is old, and there is not a man on earth to come in to us after the manner of all the world." They decide to trick Lot into impregnating them so the human race can continue. They get him drunk and then go in to "lay with" him, the elder on the first night and the younger on the second night. Genesis is careful to add that Lot "did not know when she lay down or when she rose." They both become pregnant and give birth to sons, Moab and Ammon, who go on to create the Moabite and the Ammonite nations. In Hebrew, Moab means "from the father" and Ammon means "of my people."

It should be clear that in their bed-tricks, Lot's daughters are similar to the other mothers in Abraham's family. They engage in similar strategizing to manipulate the continuation of their family's seed. However, they take it to another level entirely. They deceive their father, taking full control of the plan. Are their actions righteous and virtuous, or perverse and transgressive? Surprisingly, and unlike Sarah's case, these questions are not asked about them in the biblical story. Indeed, their story is told in a very matter-of-fact tone with no editorializing or commentary. It is only in later writings about them that they are put on trial for their actions.

But there is more. In Genesis 19, Lot's daughters, like Sarah, experience danger and sexual threat before they become mothers. They start out as part of an Abrahamic family that is saved from the destruction of Sodom by God. But before the cave, before the bed-tricks, while they are still in Sodom, they are first depicted as utterly expendable. When a violent mob of men from Sodom surround Lot's house, threatening to assault his guests (God's angels who have come to save him and the family), Lot offers up his daughters as substitute victims. It takes time for readers today to absorb this plot twist. Lot offers his daughters as substitute victims to a mob of men who wish to either rape or assault his male guests.

A natural question, especially in light of the fact that these young women will become the foremothers of Israel's greatest king, would be, "Wait . . . aren't they valuable? Virtuous? Obedient?" After all, these are the questions that were asked about Sarah. The answer depends on what you mean by "valued." It is darkly ironic that what allows Lot's daughters to be used in this terrible way by their father is precisely the high value placed on them by their culture's standards. They are, by those standards, valuable virgin daughters who have never known a man. This is why they would be considered by Lot and the mob as tempting substitute victims. Cold comfort, to be sure. Having this type of "value" is nothing more than being a thing that is bought and sold. The daughters are pawns in exchanges between men; I would add that this does not just pertain to violent transactions such as this one with the mob, but also in typical circumstances involving marriage and bride-prices.

A standard interpretation of this part of the story is that Lot's daughters are bartered for their sexual/procreative purity because Lot values the spiritual ideal of righteous hospitality to guests above his own daughters' bodies. Again, one may accept this explanation, based on a historical study of the ancient Israelite worldview, but it is hard to stomach.

On the other hand, it could also be true that, like other stories about the mothers, this story is presenting Lot's choice (and even the daughters' later choices in the cave) as questions, part of the Bible's ongoing conversation and questions about the mothers and their chosen sons. What happens when a man prizes providing hospitality over the survival of his own children? How will Abraham's seed, through his nephew, be preserved now that his disobedient foreign wife has been killed by God?

So, the daughters are presented as sexually, procreatively valuable virgin-insiders, however reprehensible their treatment by their father may seem to readers today. It is impossible not to see this as a crime, and not just for readers today. Consider the biblical story's conclusion, which forcefully resolves the questions it raises about Lot's actions. Lot's guests, the angels of God, intervene and supernaturally force back the mob, blinding them in the process, and saving Lot, his wife, and his daughters. Just as in the case of Sarah with the foreign kings and Hagar in the desert, God, through his angels, protects defenseless women.

The scene with the mob in Sodom is not the whole of the story of Lot's daughters, though, is it? You now know that their bed-tricks in the cave outside the city of Zoar prove they are anything but passive pawns. Their actions continue generations of assertive interventions by the Abrahamic mothers of the Genesis narratives, who repeatedly take matters into their own hands to conceive children of the promise. Might it be that God's approval is implied by the mothers' stories, specifically in their single-minded pursuit of motherhood? Could this be why Genesis 19:30–38 does not condemn, nor praise, Lot's daughters for their actions? As noted above, the facts of their willed incest, conception, and childbearing are simply presented at face value.

Perhaps we can look at other related passages in the Hebrew Bible, which refer to the daughters' Moabite and Ammonite descendants, since they could provide clues about how the daughters' sexual trickery was understood by other biblical authors.

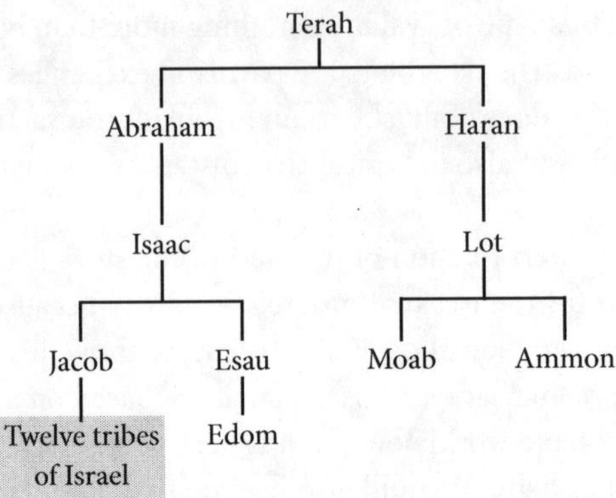

Lot's Descendants: Moabites, Ammonites, and Jesus of Nazareth

In fact, Deuteronomy 23:3–7 is a good choice. These verses prohibit Lot's Ammonite and Moabite descendants from rejoining the Israelite community to the tenth generation. The author explains the reasons. The Ammonites did not provide the weary Israelites with food and water in the desert as they made their way back from Egyptian slavery to the promised land. In addition, the king of the Moabites hired Balaam, a foreign prophet, to curse the Jewish people.

> No Ammonite or Moabite shall be admitted to the assembly of the Lord. Even to the tenth generation, none of their descendants shall be admitted to the assembly of the Lord, because they did not meet you with food and water on your journey out of Egypt, and because they hired against you Balaam son of Beor, from Pethor of Mesopotamia, to curse you. (Yet the Lord your God refused to heed Balaam; the Lord your God turned the curse into a blessing for you, because the Lord your God loved you.) You shall never promote their welfare or their prosperity as long as you live. You shall not abhor any of the Edomites, for they are your kin. You shall not abhor any of the Egyptians, because you were an alien residing in their land. The children of the third generation that are born to them may be admitted to the assembly of the Lord.

In contrast, the Edomites, Esau's hybrid-foreign branch of Abraham's family, are considered kin and only prohibited to the third generation. Why the difference? Could it be that, even though it is not stated outright, the lack of righteousness in Lot and his daughters' descendants is caused somehow, in the biblical authors' minds, by their incestuous origins?

This question may seem far-fetched, but consider that Deuteronomy 23:1–2, the verses just before the passage about the Ammonites and Moabites, begin by rejecting male sexual impotence and "illicit unions" (unlawful coitus): "No one whose testicles are crushed or whose penis is cut off shall be admitted to the assembly of the Lord. Those born of an illicit union shall not be admitted to the assembly of the Lord." Is it unrelated that the prohibition against Ammonites and Moabites entering the assembly directly follows? And why is this prohibition gender-specific to the men: Moabite and Ammonite women may enter the assembly and marry Israelite men because they are assumed not to have been responsible for either of the betrayals mentioned earlier in the passage. In other words, just how guilty *was* Lot in his incest with his daughters? How guilty were his daughters? Is it only *nonsexual* offenses committed by the Moabites and Ammonites that are directly cited in Deuteronomy 23? Are the two opening verses about male organs and illicit unions indirectly pointing to Genesis 19? Are incestuous origins at least partly responsible for the lack of moral and religious righteousness in the Ammonites and Moabites? It's difficult to know for sure. I hope it is becoming clear just how nuanced incest, mothers, sons, and righteousness become once we start looking at the Hebrew Bible as a conversation across authors and time.

Still other answers may lie in the stories of the foreign-born Davidic mothers, Tamar the Canaanite and Ruth the Moabite. For, if the Abrahamic mothers schemed and planned to ensure they would mother sons of Israel, the Davidic mothers, beginning with Lot's daughters, significantly upped the ante, deceiving the fathers of their children with greater audacity and courage.

TAMAR'S REVENGE

Tamar's story is told in chapter 38 of Genesis. The father of her twin boys is Judah, Jacob's son by Leah. In many ways, this story reads like an indictment of the men of Abraham's family and of the ways in which laws created to protect women often do not. Tamar is passed around between the men in Judah's family and then abandoned by Judah entirely, in spite of legal safety nets that should have kept her safe.

The story begins with Judah separating from his brothers, traveling to a new place, and marrying a Canaanite woman named Shua, who bears him three sons. We already know this is a problematic scenario: a chosen son of Jacob marrying a Canaanite woman? Next, Tamar, who is also a Canaanite, becomes the wife of Judah's eldest son, Er. However, Er is a wicked man and so God kills him. That Judah's son by a Canaanite woman is "wicked" might have been attributed to the ethnicity of his mother, given the view of Canaanites at the time, yet the fact of Er's wickedness and his punishment are offered with no explanation of any kind.

Now, according to Jewish law, if a husband dies, his closest male relative is encouraged to marry his wife to keep the woman and children in the extended family. Therefore, Tamar is given to Judah's second son, Onan. Onan, however, knowing that the children would legally be considered Er's and not his, avoids impregnating Tamar by withdrawing and "spilling his seed." This deeply displeases the God of miraculous conceptions, who proceeds to kill the second son of Judah. The laws that ensured maximum conception, childbearing, and abundance are thus thwarted multiple times by the men in this chosen family, beginning with Judah's marrying a "foreign" wife and ending with "spilled seed" and death. So strong is the distrust of foreign wives, however, that Judah refuses to give Tamar to his third son, Shelah, instead sending her back to her father's house. He tells her that when Shelah is grown into a man, he will send for her. Yet it is clear that he has no intention of doing so.

Distrust, half-truths, abandonment, and callous indifference to Tamar's fate thus pave the way for yet another mother's bed-trick. Tamar hears that her father-in-law is heading back home to Bethlehem and that Shelah is grown, yet she has not been sent for. In response, she seeks Judah out on the road, disguises herself as a prostitute, and tricks him into impregnating her. Before the deed, Judah gives her collateral belongings as promise that he will send payment to her later. When she becomes pregnant, the people report the scandal of his former daughter-in-law to Judah. Judah readies to punish her in the sight of the whole town, but she produces his belongings as proof that he is the father of the children in her womb. Judah is forced to confess, "She is more in the right than I, since I did not give her to my son Shelah." Thus, Tamar enters Judah's house, becoming a key foremother of King David.

For the first time in the book of Genesis, the author explicitly vindicates a mother's bed-trick, and that of a Canaanite mother, a foreign wife, no less! God intervenes in Tamar's story not to open her womb, but to punish her husbands. In the Bible itself, then, there is no condemnation of Tamar, just as there is none for Lot's daughters.

With this story, we are far beyond the legal bed-trick hatched between Sarah and her husband, Abraham. Far too from the polygamous child-making of Jacob, his wives, and their slaves. What holds Tamar back is not a womb closed by God, but the failure of the chosen fathers to follow God's laws. Tamar conceives the forefather of King David through her own desperation and righteous determination, all through sexual subterfuge that is by the norms of her day highly condemnable. And in doing so she ends up furthering God's plan for Israel.

RUTH AND NAOMI: FEMALE SOLIDARITY IN CRISIS

The final story of this chapter is that of Ruth the Moabite, to which we now return. When we interrupted her story, Ruth and her Israelite mother-in-law, Naomi, had returned to Bethlehem from Moab after their husbands' deaths and Boaz, a close relative of her late husband, was providing support to them. It only remains to describe how Ruth fits into our group of sexually audacious mothers who bring about the birth of King David. As it turns out, this too involves a bed-trick.

While the family connection between the women and Boaz is at first unknown, Naomi soon realizes who he is. Knowing the law about keeping widows in the family, she instructs Ruth to bathe, dress up, and go to Boaz at night: "uncover his feet and lie down." In the Bible, the term "foot" is often used as a metaphor for the male genitals, so it appears that Naomi is telling Ruth to seduce Boaz on the floor of his barn. This is a sexually aggressive plan, to say the least. Ruth does so, and at the same time appeals to Boaz's kinship relationship with her, telling him he is "next-of-kin," indirectly citing the law. Boaz recognizes her claim. He offers her first to another male in the family, who refuses her, after which Boaz agrees to marry her. Along with Ruth, Boaz is given a field that had belonged to Naomi's husband. His son's wife and property are transferred to Boaz as one. Ruth's incorporation into the Israelite family is complete.

What is so interesting about Ruth's story is that the female competition and mutual betrayal that characterized the other mothers' stories is absent. Here, again, we have an Israelite woman and a foreign woman at risk and in need of a man's protection, and yet they are tied together in solidarity and love. Naomi and Ruth do not abandon each other. Ruth says to Naomi, "Where you go, I will go; where you live, I will live; your people shall be my people, and your God my God." The inclusion of a foreign wife and mother within Israel is accepted in this story, which is all the more amazing since Ruth births the direct ancestor to the messiah-king of Israel, a role that was assigned exclusively to insider-wives, sisters, and cousins before.

Then again, perhaps not completely. A remnant of the preference for insider mothers may be visible in a small detail at the end of Ruth's story (Ruth 4:14–17), which explains that Ruth's child, Obed, the grandfather of King David, was labeled by the women of the neighborhood as Naomi's child:

> Then the women said to Naomi, "Blessed be the Lord, who has not left you this day without next-of-kin; and may his name be renowned in Israel! He shall be to you a restorer of life and a nourisher of your old age; for your daughter-in-law who loves you, who is more to you than seven sons, has borne him." Then Naomi took the child and laid him in her bosom and became his nurse. The women of the neighborhood gave him a name, saying, "A son has been born to Naomi."

These foremothers of King David uphold Israel in such unorthodox ways, yet are they really breaking the mold? They are more defiant and more independent than the mothers before them. Their stories make me wonder if they still depend on God at all to bring the king into being. Just who is controlling their wombs?

The insightful Hebrew scholar Ruth Kara-Ivanov Kaniel writes about the links between the Davidic mothers and those before them as follows:

> All those acts of deceit, incest, and adultery [of the earlier mothers] are acquitted through "sublimation" during Ruth's seduction of Boaz upon the threshing floor. Expressions such as "Then she came softly, and uncovered his feet, and lay down" echo back to the cave in Tzoar, where the two daughters of Lot once had prohibited relations with their father . . . The transformative sexual sins documented in the Book of Ruth indicate a gradual psychological process during which the biblical heroines work through the "trauma" that was inflicted upon them by the violence and repression they knew, and turn it into a tool of empowerment and healing.[6]

It *is* indeed tempting to see healing and empowerment in the evolving stories about the mothers, and if stories were self-contained, static things I would happily nod my head yes. Unfortunately, they are not self-contained. They do not exist on the page forever voicing one unchanging message. Instead, they continue to produce a variety of meanings as they are read by different people in different times. Because of this, Ruth's story is one voice in a conversation about women, vulnerability, sex, and desperate, compulsory motherhood, that is heard in many ways. And these ways never end, even now.

3

Mary, Matriarch of the "New" Israel, Delivers the Ultimate King

Incommensurable, unlocalizable maternal body. First there is division . . . Then another abyss opens between this body and the body that was inside it: the abyss that separates mother and child. What relationship is there between me or, more modestly, between my body and this internal graft, this crease inside, which with the cutting of the umbilical cord becomes another person, inaccessible? My body and . . . him. No relation. Nothing to do with one another . . . the abyss between me and what was mine but is now irremediably alien.

—Julia Kristeva, "Stabat Mater"

In 1977, Julia Kristeva, a brilliant Bulgarian-French philosopher, literary theorist, psychoanalyst, and feminist wrote the lines above in an essay entitled "Stabat Mater [Dolorosa]" which was published in English translation in 1985.[7] It was based on a medieval Christian hymn of the same name—"the sorrowful mother is standing"—which depicts Mary, the mother of Jesus, standing beneath the cross on which her son is put to death. Responding to the hymn, Kristeva's essay is a scholarly exploration of how maternity, or "the maternal," has been understood in Christianity through the suffering of the Virgin Mary. In her essay, Kristeva used an unusual format. She set the scholarly argument she was making about Mary in a column on the left side of the page. In a right-hand column, she placed a poetic account of her own bodily and psychological experiences of conception, gestation, birthing, and mothering.

The quote above, one of the passages in the experiential column, is powerful in the context of this chapter because it contrasts so deeply with the Christian story of Mary, offering a very different story of what mothers can and do experience. Kristeva's account is grounded in her bodily responses as she physically and psychically separates from her son at childbirth. Yet, those responses could not be further from church doctrines and early church stories about Mary. Christian doctrine was first and foremost invested in establishing Jesus' divinity. *This cannot be overstated.* In this chapter, and again in chapter 5, we will see that any genuine interest in Mary, her body, or her feelings, if any existed at all, is overridden by the need to *use* her as a proof God was made man, became flesh, and died for human sin on a Roman cross. As a result, Mary and her body had to become more like Jesus, otherworldly, asexual, pure in mind and heart. She had to become "blessed among women." Christian traditions about Mary thus sanitized her body, casting her as virginal, sinless, and ultimately deathless, her death akin to falling asleep and ascending to heaven. How else could she become worthy of birthing a god? How else to prove that Jesus is God?

I am also arguing, of course, that the Christian depiction of Mary and her desexed, obedient motherhood was a response to, and attempted resolution of, the Hebrew Bible's ambivalence about the sexuality and religious obedience of Israel's mothers. Remember that the Hebrew Bible was the sacred text of Jesus and his followers and remains so for Christians today. The mothers they knew and loved were the Hebrew Bible matriarchs. In the New Testament, furthermore, the connections are patently clear.

As we have seen in the matriarchs' stories, the mothers required God's reproductive intervention to conceive the heroes and patriarchs that built the nation of Israel and brought blessings and salvation to the Israelite sons of God. In Mary's story this "God of the womb" reappears and again works a miraculous conception in this new Israelite mother. God's intimate creation of a new people, a new Israel, also depends on an empty womb upon which God must act. However, unlike Kristeva's free expression of maternal ambivalence and anxiety about where she as a mother begins and her son ends, and even unlike the Hebrew Bible mothers' desperate and often sexually charged procreative schemes, Mary's story presents an obedient, self-erasing, sanitized virgin mother: "Here am I, the servant of the Lord; let it be with me according to your word."

Mary's place in the lineage of Israel's mothers, and how she functions as a revision or fulfillment of them, religiously and biologically, is the focus of this chapter. Make no mistake, the story of Jesus (and his mother) in the New Testament is still a Jewish story, one that grew out of, and was presented as fulfilling, Jewish history and hopes. If we consider the first-century world in which the New Testament was written, this makes a great deal of sense. The relationships and identities of Jews who remained traditional in their beliefs and practices and Jews who followed Jesus were extremely close and fluid. In ancient Mediterranean cities, the lives of traditional Jews, Jewish Christians, Pagans, and Gentile Christians were deeply intertwined.

This can be seen in the New Testament itself, in which Jesus preaches in synagogues and quotes the Hebrew Bible to support his understanding of Jewish law. In the Acts of the Apostles, the apostles James and Peter continue to go to the Jerusalem temple after Jesus dies and is resurrected. There are Pharisees among the elder decision-makers at the first Christian council in Jerusalem around 50 CE.

The deep connections between Jews and Christians extends further, as is evident in early Christian sermons, as late as the fourth century, that include reprimands and angry warnings to those Christians who still attended Jewish festivals. Such sermons, especially eight that were preached at Antioch by the "honey-mouthed" bishop John Chrysostom, were filled with virulent anti-Jewish rants that dehumanized traditional Jews and denounced their religious practices. Chrysostom and others of his ilk preached and enforced segregation between Christians and Jews.[8] What can we deduce from his angry attacks? It is simple. Christians in Antioch were still attending Jewish festivals. And there is more. Christians gave their children biblical names, like Abraham and Jacob. Jews had been waiting for the return of the messiah since the Davidic monarchy collapsed. First-century Jewish Christians believed Jesus was that messiah. Details about his mother, Mary, would therefore have registered in both Jewish and Christian minds as building on the stories of Israel's mothers, whether people saw her as a distortion, fulfillment, or replacement of them.

With all that said, it may seem surprising that in the New Testament itself, Mary's presence and voice are scarce. Like her Hebrew Bible foremothers, her story is above all the story of her son. In the Gospels of Matthew and Luke, Mary is mentioned in the following eight scenes: 1) an annunciation scene where the angel Gabriel tells her that she will conceive Jesus; 2) a visit to her cousin Elizabeth and her song in praise of God, the *Magnificat* ("My soul magnifies the Lord"); 3) an escape to Egypt (in Matthew's Gospel only) to keep Jesus safe from King Herod; 4) the birth of Jesus; 5) scenes related to Jesus' adolescent presentation in the temple; 6) three scenes during Jesus' ministry; 7) the crucifixion; and 8) the coming of the Holy Spirit at Pentecost in Jerusalem after Jesus' death.

She speaks in just four—only half of her scenes. The first time is during the annunciation, when Mary questions the angel Gabriel about the mechanics of her conception of Jesus: "How can this be, since I am a virgin?" The second is when she sings the *Magnificat* praising God and linking herself and her son to the covenant with Abraham and Israel. In these two instances, Mary seems to be trying to understand her miraculous conception of Jesus. Then, in the Jerusalem temple she rebukes Jesus for staying behind at the temple and ignoring his obligation to his earthly parents. Later, at a wedding in Cana she tells Jesus that the wine has run out, and then tells those nearby to, "do whatever he tells you." In these two scenes, Mary seems to move from seeing Jesus as an earthly son to seeing him as a miracle-worker. Unfortunately, that is all that Mary says. Other than these, Mary is said to respond internally to what Jesus himself and others say about him: "Mary treasured all these words and pondered them in her heart." Yet we are not privy to her thoughts. That she "treasures" words about Jesus suggests she is perhaps proud of, or grateful for, her son. There is also the possibility that this hints at a deepening understanding in Mary of who or what he is. Unfortunately, the text is too coy for us to do anything but speculate. In the end, Mary is not the focus; she is a prop that defines Jesus.

As a result, the primary link between Mary and the Hebrew Bible mothers is found not in scheming or bed-tricks or a desperate desire for children, but in her miraculous conception. Of all the miraculous conceptions in the Bible, the Gospel of Luke provides the most detailed description of this miracle, even as it builds on those that went before. In his opening chapter, Luke recounts how the angel Gabriel announces to Mary that she will conceive Jesus. In this annunciation, we find a creative appropriation and elaboration of several details presented in the Genesis account of the angels' visit to Abraham and Sarah at Mamre. These include: 1) an angelic annunciation of a miracle child, 2) a mother's response to the angel's message, and 3) as I've said, more details than any found in any Hebrew Bible miraculous conception, in this case of the mechanics of Mary's conception of Jesus and what God does to bring it about.

Parallels and echoes of Sarah's encounter with the angel(s) abound. The angel Gabriel comes to Mary in Nazareth, while in Genesis 18, three angels come to Abraham and Sarah at Mamre. In Genesis, it is Abraham who receives the announcement of a miraculous conception just as Joseph does in the Gospel of Matthew. (Matthew's account thus differs from Luke's account of the annunciation to Mary alone.) Still, in Genesis 18, Sarah is also listening, just as Mary is listening in the first chapter of the Gospel of Luke. The angel announces that in a year Sarah will have a son, and while conception is not explicitly described at Mamre, three chapters later, Genesis

21:1–2 describes Sarah's conception during a second visit: "The Lord visited Sarah as he had said, and the Lord did to/for Sarah as he had spoken. And Sarah conceived and bore a son for Abraham."[9]

During the Genesis annunciation, Sarah has difficulty understanding God's intended action. So, too, Mary is confused by Gabriel's statement, "the Lord is with you." Some scholars have suggested that Mary (and New Testament readers) could have understood the phrase, "the Lord is with you" as a signal that Jesus was already conceived within Mary. It could have signified that Jesus' conception in Mary had occurred precisely at the time of the angel's greeting. (Indeed, this idea was taken up by later Christian authors.) Luke's words, however, are ambiguous. At Luke 1:31–33, the angel Gabriel takes the conversation in another direction, calming Mary's confusion, telling her that her child is a descendant of the great King David and that he will inherit God's covenant and the monarchy:

> And now, you will conceive in your womb and bear a son, and you will name him Jesus. He will be great and will be called the Son of the Most High, and the Lord God will give to him the throne of his ancestor David. He will reign over the house of Jacob forever, and of his kingdom there will be no end.

Gabriel explains to Mary that God's intervention in her miraculous conception proves that "God's promises never fail" (Luke 1:37). This not only defines Jesus' birth as the fulfillment of God's covenant with his chosen people, but it also parallels the Genesis angel's statement to Sarah that nothing is impossible for the Lord (18:14).

Looking at these two annunciation scenes together, a striking revision is also apparent. At first Mary acts like Sarah. She is confused and questions the possibility of such a conception: "How can this be, since I am a virgin?" (Luke 1:34). This echoes Sarah's skeptical question: "After I have grown old, and my husband is old, shall I have pleasure?" (Genesis 18:12). Yet Mary has two additional responses to the angel's message, beyond the original doubt she shares with Sarah. The first is her submissive, obedient acceptance of God's action on her womb quoted above. The second is the *Magnificat,* in which she sings praises to God, evoking Israelite history and placing herself and her son squarely within God's plan for Israel. It is worth quoting the full passage (Luke 1:46–55), so that the deep links to the Hebrew Bible frame are fully appreciated:

> My soul magnifies the Lord, and my spirit rejoices in God my Savior,
> for he has looked with favor on the lowliness of his servant.
> Surely, from now on all generations will call me blessed;

> for the Mighty One has done great things for me, and holy is his name.
> His mercy is for those who fear him from generation to generation.
> He has shown strength with his arm; he has scattered the proud in the thoughts of their hearts.
> He has brought down the powerful from their thrones, and lifted up the lowly;
> he has filled the hungry with good things, and sent the rich away empty.
> He has helped his servant Israel, in remembrance of his mercy,
> according to the promise he made to our ancestors, to Abraham and to his descendants forever.

Thus, Mary jubilantly affirms at the end of the *Magnificat* that the birth of her son is a sign of God's promise of "mercy to Abraham and his descendants forever." The song repeatedly draws distinctions between the many who oppress God's people ("the proud," "the powerful," "the rich") and the Israelites, "God's servants." The final lines make the explicit link to Israel and the patriarchs. They establish the Genesis roots of Mary's story and affirm God's role in the conception and continuing nurture of his (new) chosen people.

Another way that Mary's conception of Jesus in Luke elaborates upon the matriarchs' miraculous conceptions is the detailed description Luke provides of *how* Jesus is conceived. Luke 1:35 describes the process as follows: "The angel said to her, 'A holy spirit will come upon you, and the power of the Most High will overshadow you; therefore the child to be born will be holy; he will be called Son of God.'" This is a much more developed picture of God's actions on a mother's womb. Compare the language used to describe the Hebrew Bible's conceptions: God did as he promised, heard and granted prayers, opened wombs, and made mothers conceive. These are devoid of any clarifying details.

In contrast, Luke introduces two new actors (or agents) into the process of Mary's conception: a holy spirit and a power of God. To understand these from within Jewish tradition, we should note that this "holy spirit" could have been understood as an angelic spirit, a spirit of inspiration, or God's creative (begetting) spirit, such as that which hovered over the waters at the creation of the world in Genesis 1. These are important historical understandings of the word "spirit." As the church has evolved, the spirit in Luke 1:45 has been understood through the lens of the doctrine of "the Trinity" or the "three persons" of God (Father, Son, and Holy Spirit). However, this doctrine had not been developed when the New Testament was written, so understanding "a holy spirit" as *the* Holy Spirit of the Trinity is to read back into the text from later church doctrine.

A lot of scholarly attention has also been paid to the verb that is used to describe what the "power of God" actually does to Mary. In Greek, it is ἐπισκιάσει, which, transliterated into the English alphabet, is pronounced "episkiazei." Elsewhere in the New Testament this same verb is used to describe the apostle Peter's shadow, which heals the sick. In the Greek translation of the Hebrew Bible, it was also used to communicate God's protective care, the hovering of God's spirit over the void at creation, and God's dwelling in a tent in the desert, accompanying the Israelites in their flight from Egypt to the promised land.[10] So Luke could be using this verb, which is most often translated as "overshadow" in contemporary editions of the New Testament, to signify healing, protecting, creating, or residing within. It is hard to know what meaning is preferable.

Why do such details matter? The answer is that they establish what the mother (in this case, Mary) actually contributes to the conception of her child. If a woman slyly manipulates a man into impregnating her, as Lot's daughters and Tamar did, she actively participates in—one might even say she determines—the creation of the chosen people and their messiahs. If a woman passively is acted upon, as in the case of Mary, then she is an obedient vessel and significantly different from her Hebrew Bible foremothers. It is true that Mary does verbally assent to God's plan for her ("Here am I, the servant of the Lord"). Much is made of this by scholars, including defining assent as exemplary obedience and submission to God. It may occur to you, as it has to me, that this is just the sort of obedient submission that was expected of Sarah when she received her angelic announcement, and that when it did not materialize—when she did not express wonder and awe at God's power—she was reprimanded.

But not so Mary. Mary does not demonstrate any dangerous sexual allure as Tamar did; she does not exhibit any sexual desire as Sarah did; nor is she driven by an existential desire to conceive and attain the status of an Israelite matriarch. She does not trick her way into the family. She is no outsider, but rather from the tribe of David according to multiple early Christian writings (if not the New Testament itself).[11] She is selfless, submissive, and obedient. She does not seek to gain control over her own reproductive choices. Through this characterization, I hope it is clear how she could be seen as a poster girl for the most idealized version of the Hebrew Bible matriarchs—or perhaps even infinitely superior to them. I hope it is also clear how her characterization has contributed to current ambivalent attitudes towards sexuality, including fear of women's desire, the continued desexualizing, sanitizing, and idealizing of selfless motherhood, and current secular and religious laws governing reproductive rights, such as birth control and abortion. Luke's Mary stands as an impossible ideal that has been leveraged as a powerful control over Christian women's behaviors and identities.

But hold on! There are other versions of Mary's conception in the early church that offer other visions of who and what Mary is. For early Christianity was not even remotely uniform in the early centuries. Jews, Gentiles, Syrians, Africans, Romans, people from the West and the East were all followers of Jesus. Their ideas about who Jesus was and how he came into their world were incredibly diverse.

THE HUMAN MARY AND THE DIVINE MATERNAL

I want to start this section with a poem entitled *Christmas Poem*. It was written by Kaitlin Hardy Shetler, an advocate for women's rights who also occasionally preaches to Christian congregations. She posted the poem online in December of 2019 and the post was subsequently shared over 30,000 times. This is not to mention the many repostings of the poem that have been shared as much and more, making its impact considerable indeed. Shetler's depiction of Mary's motherhood, understood in pointedly physical and female terms, and her challenge to how it is suppressed today in many churches (particularly Protestant churches), clearly resonated with people. The poem is, in my view, a perfect way to introduce the second-century descriptions of Mary's conception of Jesus below. They too are detailed and embodied. Shetler's poem goes like this:

> sometimes I wonder
> if Mary breastfed Jesus
> if she cried out when he bit her
> or if she sobbed when he would not latch.
> and sometimes I wonder
> if this is all too vulgar
> to ask in a church
> full of men
> without milk stains on their shirts
> or coconut oil on their breasts
> preaching from pulpits off limits to the Mother of God.
> but then I think of feeding Jesus,
> birthing Jesus,
> the expulsion of blood
> and smell of sweat,
> the salt of a mother's tears
> onto the soft head of the Salt of the Earth,

feeling lonely
and tired
hungry
annoyed
overwhelmed
loving
and I think,
if the vulgarity of birth is not
honestly preached
by men who carry power but not burden,
who carry privilege but not labor,
who carry authority but not submission,
then it should not be preached at all.
because the real scandal of the Birth of God
lies in the cracked nipples of a
14 year old
and not in the sermons of ministers
who say women
are too delicate
to lead.

From this vantage point, then, let's look at two second-century Christian texts entitled *Odes of Solomon* and *Sibylline Oracles*. The first is a collection of very early Christian hymns (odes) and the second is a series of Jewish-Christian prophecies. Ode 19 and Oracle 8 will be our focus since they each elaborate on God's participation in Mary's conception, birthing, and—yes—breastfeeding of Jesus! These texts significantly expand upon the description of conception in the first chapter of Luke. In them, Mary's body joins with several celestial beings, including God, Jesus in the form of an angel, a holy spirit, and archangels to conceive Jesus.

Perhaps not surprisingly, these retellings of the conception and birth of Jesus were not appreciated by the church leaders of the emerging orthodox church. They preached sexual abstinence in marriage, and virginity out of marriage. In their writings, it appears that the physical details of the maternal body were deeply disturbing to them. This is evident in their negative descriptions of "dripping breasts" and "stinking wombs."

Regrettably, their attitudes can be compared to influential scholars today who have described the accounts of Jesus' conception in Ode 19 as "grotesque" and void of any sophisticated theological thought.[12] In dismissing alternate accounts of the conception of Jesus like Ode 19, such scholars reveal the same deep discomfort with, and resistance to, embodiment that the early church fathers expressed. Just as Shetler sets her woman's vision of Mary's conception and birthing over and against attitudes about women and women's bodies in many churches today, so Ode 19 and Oracle 8 apparently contradict today's scholars' "sophisticated" reconstruction of early Christian beliefs.

Let us try, instead, to meet these texts on their own terms, starting with the *Odes of Solomon.* The odes are an amazing collection of very early Christian hymns. As the title indicates, they were attributed to King Solomon, who ruled Israel from approximately 970 to 931 BCE. However, based on the language used and historical clues within the text, scholars have concluded that the hymns were actually written around 100 CE or shortly thereafter in Antioch (present-day Syria). Most scholars agree that the language in which they were originally written was second-century Syriac and not the tenth-century BCE Hebrew of Solomon. So, what's with the title?

The fact is that many texts written in the early centuries of the church were attributed to the most respected and holy men of their tradition, some of them long since dead. One of the most obvious examples is *The Apocalypse of Adam*, which describes a vision that Adam, the first human being, had of the end of the world. It was written between the first and second centuries CE (at roughly the same time as the *Odes of Solomon*). If Adam wrote this text, he would have enjoyed quite a life span, and yet what he would have known and understood by then would have been immeasurable, no? As for King Solomon and his "authorship" of the *Odes*, he was known for his wisdom and justice, so any hymns written by him would be greatly respected. Teachings by Adam or Solomon would have been seen as extremely authoritative. Scholars struggle to explain this practice of attributing texts to religious figures long dead. Did the authors do this simply to enhance the authority of their texts? Did they believe they were reinterpreting previous visions, wisdom, religious experiences, and teachings? Did they have ecstatic experiences that they believed took them into the minds and hearts of their traditions' holiest men? We just do not know.

What we do know is that the form of Christianity in Syria in the early second century was a very Jewish Christianity, one that held to, and built upon, the Jewish roots of Jesus and his teachings. This is borne out in the *Odes.* Just as Jewish tradition offered a teaching known as "the Two Ways"—one of life (Torah observance) and one of death (sin and apostasy)—so the hymns starkly differentiate between those who are walking in "the Way of Truth" and those who are not. As second-century Jews awaited their messiah hopefully, the hymns ecstatically rejoice that the Messiah has come. For these reasons, the hymns represent just the kind of continuity and embellishment of Jewish stories and beliefs that we are exploring as we connect the stories of the Hebrew Bible mothers and Mary.

It is the nineteenth ode that describes Mary's conception of Jesus, and its account departs significantly from Luke's. To begin with, in Ode 19 Jesus is conceived in heaven before he enters Mary's body. The conception is followed by an account of Mary's labor and birthing of Jesus. Note that the odist is the "I," the one who is speaking, in this ode. He describes Jesus' conception as what can only be described as an auto-insemination enacted in heaven. The milk (semen?) of God is milked from God's breasts by a holy spirit *who takes it into her womb*, so that it will not be "spilt" without purpose. That holy spirit then "gives" this milk to the world, which is unaware of the gift. Mary's womb, however, "catches it" and she conceives and gives birth to Jesus. Here is the text:

> A cup of milk was offered to me
> And I drank it with the sweetness of the Lord's kindness.
> The Son is the cup, and the Father is He who was milked, and the Holy Spirit is She who milked Him because His breasts were full
> And it was undesirable that His milk should be spilt without purpose.
> The Holy Spirit opened her [own] womb
> And mixed the milk of the two breasts of the Father
> And gave the mixture to the world without their knowing.
> And those who take [it] are in the perfection of the right hand.
> The womb of the Virgin caught it
> and she received conception and gave birth.
> And the Virgin became a mother through great mercy
> And she labored and bore a Son without suffering pain
> Because it did not happen without purpose.
> And she did not require a midwife because He delivered Her.
> As a man she bore by will, and she bore with display,
> And acquired [her Son] with great power.
> And she loved him with redemption
> And guarded him with kindness,
> And showed him with greatness. Hallelujah.[13]

Notice how Mary's considerable power as she goes through labor and delivery are closely blended with God's procreative power. God and the heavenly spirit initially provide milk and womb, conceiving "milk" which Mary's womb then "catches." Then she, in turn, conceives Jesus. Mary does not need a midwife and suffers no pain in childbirth because God is her midwife. She bears her child like a strong man, with a male will, and "with great power."

So many questions arise in this blending of heavenly and bodily procreation, especially about its gendered language and imagery. Is Mary male? Is God female? Is it Mary, a holy spirit, or God that conceives and delivers Jesus? The image of God supplying milk (semen?) to Mary's womb (even if via a spirit) is clearly one that did not appear in more orthodox Christian texts. Who is this holy spirit with a womb? Remember this text is written centuries before the orthodox doctrine of the Trinity is defined, so defining this holy spirit as God (a part of the Trinity) is complicated to say the least. This could be an embryonic form of what would eventually become the doctrine of the Trinity, but here such an understanding is not even close to fully formed.

Some scholars have argued that Mary is "made male" in Ode 19, "bearing as a man and not as a woman in pain."[14] They argue that the passage in question takes away Mary's female procreative power and gives it to God, who has breasts and milk. However, I see the passage very differently. In it I see a remarkable continuum of gender fluidity (a fusion of male and female power) that is imaged in a continuous divine-human womb. In this way, God's involvement in (pro)creating a new elect and a new Israel is presented in both heavenly and very physical detail. As for Mary being male, or made secondary to God, the nature of the verbs ascribed to Mary in this ode belies such an interpretation. Consider that her actions are quintessentially female and biological, involving womb, labor, birthing, love, and protection. Her womb catches the heavenly milk; she gives birth; she labors and bears her child; she loves, guards, and shows him to the world. These are not male acts, certainly not by ancient standards. Neither is she a passive receptacle, even considering the divine auto-conception of Jesus that precedes her bodily role. There is no either/or in this text. This ode describes a fusion or extension of the maternal womb. The spirit's and Mary's wombs are virtually one, both catching God's "milk." This is quite an elaboration of Luke's Gospel.

In light of our overarching questions about how the biblical mothers' miraculous conceptions establish their children as chosen sons of God, I want to think about how the *Odes* do this. Perhaps Ode 19's conception narrative relates to the *Odes'* focus on differentiating between those who walk in "the Way of Truth" and those who walk in "Error." In what way does the divine-human conception described in Ode 19 legitimize a new chosen people? How does it establish a new elect or new Israel, as the Hebrew Bible mothers before Mary had done for Israel?

One way to approach this question is to ask *what* or *who* is being conceived in Ode 19. In fact, what does God "conceive"—and mother—*across all the Odes* in the hymnbook? Remember that in Genesis, Israel is initially born out of the miracle of a son of the covenant, conceived post-menopause, and breastfed by Sarah, a God-rejuvenated human mother. Abraham's and Sarah's God is a father, not a mother, and yet . . . Their God promises his descendants land, children, abundant food, and wealth, protecting them from famine (feeding) and promising them many offspring (conception). Those are actually quite maternal functions: feeding, protecting, providing children . . . How does the God of the *Odes of Solomon* compare? How does s/he bless his/her new Christian sons? Let's start with God's milk.

In 1980, the insightful biblical scholar Hans Drijvers did a comparative analysis across all the odes trying to figure out what God's "milk" symbolizes in this hymn. He determined that God's milk, described in Ode 19 as "the sweetness of the Lord's kindness," is a symbol for God's grace and mercy—the very thing that brings about human salvation. Jesus is the cup, the means of offering that grace and mercy. It follows then that what is conceived and delivered in Ode 19 is kindness, grace, and salvation in the form of breast milk, which the odist drinks.

The divine-human conception of Jesus is achieved through the milk of a maternal God; the same milk that fills Mary's womb is then fed also to the odist. That is not all, however. That milk-salvation is also fed to all Christians in other hymns, creating a new, saved, people. For instance, in Ode 8, all Christians gain access to God's milk *in their mothers' human wombs* and this is established through a parallel Hebrew Bible passage. This becomes explicit when, in Ode 8, Jesus describes his new "elect ones" (chosen ones) using images and language from Psalm 139 in the Hebrew Bible. In the Hebrew Bible psalm (also a hymn), King David sings to God:

> For it was you who formed my inward parts;
> you knit me together in my mother's womb.
> I praise you, for I am fearfully and wonderfully made. Wonderful are your works; that I know very well.
> My frame was not hidden from you,
> when I was being made in secret,
> intricately woven in the depths of the earth.
> Your eyes beheld my unformed substance.

Here is the excerpt from Ode 8 in which Christ describes new Christian sons:

> And before they had existed,
> I recognized them
> And imprinted a seal on their faces.
> I fashioned their members,
> And my own breasts I prepared for them,
> That they might drink my holy milk and live by it.[15]

This blending of Hebrew Bible and Jewish-Christian hymns makes explicit God's/Jesus' presence in, and action on, the *human* maternal womb. That is not all. The ode goes on to describe continued nurture through God's breasts. God co-conceives and breastfeeds all Christian sons of God before and after they are born. The actions of God described in Psalm 139 are here made explicitly maternal. God acts on Mary's womb and now on all Christian mothers' wombs. The *Odes* do not offer the miracle of a son of the promise breastfed by a God-rejuvenated human mother; instead, God becomes the mother and breastfeeds all Christian sons of God. They are the work of God's will and creative fashioning, through the medium of divine milk: "I willed and fashioned mind and heart; and they are my own."[38]

In the *Odes*, then, the maternal womb, through God's interventions, is extended, pervasive, and salvific. It—and Mary herself—exists on a continuum of divine maternal birthing and nurture that includes God's breast, the Holy Spirit's womb, Mary's womb, and Jesus as cup. What is ultimately birthed by this divine-human maternal body is Christians and, ultimately, the elect church. Note that Mary is not barren as her foremothers were. She is not particularly virginal either. She is simply in perfect, active harmony of body and will with God.

Odes of Solomon 19 is just one of many visions of Mary's motherhood. *Sibylline Oracle* 8 offers another unexpected and unorthodox account of the conception of Jesus. It is similar to Luke's account in that it features an angelic annunciation. However, in other ways it aligns more with Ode 19. For instance, it too describes a pre-Mary, heavenly conception, even if it is quite different than the one in Ode 19. Also, like Ode 19, Oracle 8 makes use of explicit Hebrew Bible narratives and themes. To begin with, the Oracle describes Jesus as a new Moses, "the staff of David," and "the stone he [God] promised."[16] These Hebrew Bible images once again serve to reinforce the continuity of God's interventions on behalf of God's people, from Israelites to newly born Christians.

Once Jesus' continuity with Hebrew Bible patriarchs and prophecies has been established, a description of Jesus' heavenly conception follows. In the description, an odd collapsing of time takes place in which the Genesis creation narrative is rewritten. It now includes God and Jesus shaping Jesus' form at the same time that they together create humanity. In this version of the Genesis creation story, Jesus is in heaven with God; he already (always?) exists. God refers to him as his "child" and commands him to create human beings ("mortal tribes") in their image:

> For the universal ruler took him [Jesus] into his counsel
> First of all in the beginning and said, "Let us both, child,

> Make mortal tribes, copying our likeness.
> Now I with my hands, then you with a word, will tend
> Our form so that we may produce a common construct."
> Mindful therefore of this resolution he will come to creation
> Bearing a corresponding copy to the holy virgin.[17]

The language and ideas in this passage are complicated and abstract. Looking at the first three lines, we see that God and Jesus create humanity in their shared image, "copying our likeness." The word for likeness also means "image," so humanity apparently *looks like* or may *be like* God and Jesus. In the next two lines, God refers to "our form" and how he and Jesus will "tend it" and together create "a common construct." This is very abstract. It seems the divine "form" that God and Jesus share will become something "constructed" that they also share. This constructed thing is presumably Jesus' divine essence or being, because, in the last two lines, the author explains that Jesus will bear "a corresponding copy" of his created form to Mary as he "comes to creation."

In this way, Oracle 8 offers a pre-Mary conception process in the celestial realm like that found in Ode 19, even if a much less embodied version. Instead of breasts and wombs, Oracle 8 uses images of likenesses, forms, constructs, and copies. Jesus' divine being is conceived in these terms. Only after this heavenly conception has been established does the oracle provide additional details about the role of Mary and her womb. Again, even Mary's labor and birth are less embodied than in Ode 19. For instance, Jesus is figured as "a new light arising from the womb of the Virgin Mary"; a light defined as language, word, and knowledge even as it puts on "mortal form." Light arising as language is certainly less embodied and less maternal than the images in Ode 19.

In between these two scenes, however, before Jesus is actually born, the heavenly "construct" (divine thought, word, or language) shaped by God and Jesus is brought to Mary's body in an annunciation scene, like that of Luke 1. Even as the text moves to the maternal body, speech and word are dominant metaphors rather than semen, milk, and wombs. The archangel Gabriel appears to Mary and speaks to her. In the exchange, Mary's response is described as both intensely physical and spiritual.[18] She is first penetrated by the breath ("grace") of God, then responds in a very physical, arguably erotic fashion including fear, wonder, trembling, a fluttering mind, a shaken heart, joy, laughter, blushing cheeks, enchantment, and awe as she "listens" to the "voice" and "word" within her:

> The archangel also addressed the maiden in speech: "Receive God, Virgin, in your immaculate womb." Thus speaking, he

> breathed in the grace of God, even to one who was always a maiden. Fear and, at the same time, wonder seized her as she listened. She stood trembling. Her mind fluttered while her heart was shaken by the unfamiliar things she heard. But again she rejoiced, and her heart was healed by the voice. The maiden laughed and reddened her cheek. . . . A word flew to her womb. In time it was made flesh and came to life in the womb and was fashioned in mortal form and became a boy by virgin birth.[19]

The "grace of God" is here figured as breath emerging from the archangel Gabriel and entering Mary. I would like to pause here and comment on the sexual undertones of this text, since I can imagine a variety of present-day responses to it. I myself find it difficult to comment on the eroticization of the penetration of Mary in Oracle 8. On the one hand, I feel relieved that Mary actually has a body, bodily responses, pleasure, joy, trembling, and laughter, because all that feels much truer to the experiences of womanhood and motherhood that I see as valuable and authentic. That is to say, it is less disturbing, at least to me, than the virginal, asexual, submissive "servant" that she is in the New Testament. On the other hand, Mary gives no consent in Oracle 8. An angel appears and orders her to "receive God" in her womb and she is described as feeling great pleasure, and I think that this could trigger a double response for many women. Christian leaders and scholars explain that Mary's pleasure is spiritual. It is the great joy of communion with the divine. We are well aware of this reading. The spiritualization of religious experience at the expense of the body is core to Christian teachings. The eroticization of mystical communion with God, however, is an equally powerful theme, particularly in the writings of medieval women mystics. That theme did not come out of thin air. It is perfectly feasible that women reading this text today may see it as essentially pornographic, too much like a male fantasy. As a scholar I would argue that these are twenty-first-century responses to a second-century oracle that was interested in altogether different questions, questions about the relationship between spirit and flesh and who or what Jesus was. In this book, however, I acknowledge the multilayered experience that reading the Bible actually provokes. For some readers, such historicizing cannot take away their visceral resistance to the penetration of a young virginal woman, insisting that she is feeling pleasure.

This leads me to ask: would the question of *what or who* is penetrating Mary make any difference? Is the "grace of God"/breath that penetrates Mary in Oracle 8 a holy spirit as in Luke and Ode 19? Who places the "grace of God" in Mary's womb? Is it a spirit working on its own? The angel Gabriel? Are there two agents of conception or one? Remember that there are three names used for the impregnating agent in Luke's account: Gabriel, a holy spirit, and the power of God. Spirit and power often accompany each other in the Hebrew Bible and New Testament but appear to be separate in many instances.

One detail may help in answering these questions. Recall that this oracle's account of Jesus' conception began with a conversation between a preexistent Christ and God, with the idea that Jesus himself would bear "a corresponding copy" of his/God's image to Mary. Is the angel, then, Jesus? Or, is the breath Jesus? Can Jesus be the angel of the annunciation in his own conception in his mother's body? What would that mean?

Let's take a minute here because a little bit of context may help to unpack these questions in an informed way. For instance, we know that Jesus is depicted as an angel in many writings of this period. In those writings, Jesus is sometimes understood as one of seven archangels, sometimes as a "thwarting angel" who battles demons, sometimes as an angel closely related to a pre-Trinity holy spirit, and sometimes identified with the archangel Michael. Often Christ, Michael, and the holy spirit run together or are fused.[20] These popular early church ideas about Jesus suggest that the possibility of Jesus bearing himself in angelic form to Mary would not have been as foreign to a second-century audience as it likely feels to readers of the New Testament today.

Let's look at an example of a closely related description of Jesus' conception that appears in a fourth-century sermon by a bishop in Jerusalem named Cyril.[21] Cyril's sermon presents, if not a fusion of Christ and an angel, then at least their actions fused. In this account, the continuum of actors that conceive Jesus is comprised of Christ, God the Father, a mighty power, who is called Michael, who is also called Mary, who has a womb . . . Fasten your seat belt:

> It is written in the [Gospel] of the Hebrews that when Christ wished to come upon the earth to men the Good Father called a mighty "power" in the heavens which was called "Michael," and committed Christ to the care thereof. And the "power" came down into the world, *and it was called Mary*, and Christ was in her womb for seven months.[22]

The fact that Mary is made synonymous with "the power" Michael in this fragment is a categorical departure. It is certainly more provocative than any correlation that could be drawn between Christ and the announcing angel. It is also quite reminiscent of the continuum of divine-human conception and nurture established between Mary and God in Ode 19. In fact, it takes that idea one step further, making Mary herself a celestial "power." No wonder Cyril denounced this account roundly in his fourth-century Christian sermon! In all the descriptions of the host of celestial actors who collaborate with Mary in Jesus' conception, this claims the greatest agency for Mary. She is (one with) a "power," possibly the angel Michael. This is interesting indeed because in the case of this text, this would mean it is *Mary* who penetrates herself during the conception! That certainly triggers a double take in our twenty-first-century responses.

Yet, celestial power is not the only attribute of Mary in Oracle 8. While other contemporary depictions as Cyril's present Mary in a completely new way, Oracle 8 does not neglect the humanity of Mary and Jesus. Mary's human body and Jesus' mortal form are equally important to the author of Oracle 8. As we have noted, at the point of conception Mary's physical reactions are pronouncedly visible. This attests to the physicality of the transmission, but also emphasizes the categorical difference between the Christ-angel and the human-Jesus and his mother. A *human* maternal womb is the medium for the creation of the son of God, who is both human and more than human.

In this way, Mary is linked back to her Hebrew Bible foremothers, for Mary's female body, so visible in her fluttering blushes and trembling limbs, also carries an echo of Sarah's response to the angelic visitors in Genesis 18. Specifically, both Mary and Sarah are described as laughing at their bodily plights. In Sarah's laugh, the limits of her postmenopausal womb are acknowledged. In contrast, Mary's laughter, interpreted in the most positive way possible, recognizes not the limits of her virginal womb, but its new miraculous capacity. Both draw attention to God's intervention in the conception of their sons.

Still, more broadly, the shifting ground upon which Jesus, "power," angel, and Mary produce her son was fertile ground, as still more second-century writings bear witness. Just as it is Christ himself who "bears a corresponding copy" of his (and God's) image to Mary in Oracle 8, we find the same idea in yet another second-century writing. The *Letter of the Apostles* presents a dialogue between the disciples and Jesus in which Jesus explains that it was he himself who came to Mary in the form of the angel Gabriel. In this text, the disciples describe the conversation as follows:

> [Jesus:] "For you know that the angel Gabriel brought the message to Mary."
>
> We answered, "Yes, O Lord."
>
> Then he answered and said to us, "Do you not then remember that I previously said to you that I became an angel to the angels?"

> And we said to him, "Yes, O Lord."
>
> And he said to us, "At that time I appeared in the form of the archangel Gabriel to [the virgin] Mary and spoke with her, and her heart received [me]; she believed and laughed; and I, the Word, went into her and became flesh; and I myself was servant for myself, and in the form of the image of an angel; so I will do after I have gone to my Father."[23]

Here Jesus is not only the angel Gabriel, but he actually conceives himself ("I went into her and became flesh"). Jesus is the one who penetrates Mary. This continuum between God, preexistent Jesus, angel, and Mary should by now be familiar. Note also again in this text, the laughter of Mary, echoing Sarah in Genesis 18 and the Mary of Ode 19.

In summary, then, Oracle 8 describes a complex continuum of (pro) creation that journeys from God's hands and Jesus' word to their "likeness" or "image," becomes a shared "construct" or "thought" that an angelic Christ breathes into Mary as a word. That "word" then flies into her womb and becomes flesh, as a boy. We have also seen that comparable texts from the same period also feature Jesus as either "in the care of" an (angelic) power (Michael or Mary?) or "in the form of the archangel Gabriel," presenting a Jesus who is both preexistent, powerful, and angelic *and* a human boy. In other words, not a traditional son of God, not a traditional patriarch, like Isaac or Jacob. The Hebrew Bible God-of-the-Womb has certainly changed too.

Compared to the God of the Hebrew Bible who opens barren wombs by fiat, we find in these early Jewish-Christian stories of Mary and Jesus a God who bridges the divine and the human, the male and the female, in much more physical and intimate ways. The God-of-the-Womb continues to bring about miraculous conceptions, just as he does in the Hebrew Bible. However, in these stories God, Mary, and Jesus merge in the process of conception in fundamental and explicit ways. To what end, you may ask? Is it not to establish a categorically different son of God in these second-century texts—and in the New Testament—a son who would have been seen as the ultimate Hebrew Bible patriarch or king, one who would eventually be defined as divine?

Before we move on to Part II and the next chapter, we must now return to the question of the mothers' role in defining chosen or elect peoples and ask how the conception stories we have looked at here establish not just Jesus, but all Christians as chosen, or elect, sons of God. How do they distinguish all Christians from all other peoples around them? How do these stories extend the Hebrew Bible narrative of a chosen people, now transformed into new sons of God, a new Israel? There are only a few clues in Oracle 8 that are relevant to this question, but they are consistent with the kinds of logic we saw in the Hebrew Bible stories.

First, from the very start, God and Christ plan to create not just Jesus in their "likeness," but also "mortal tribes," in whom Jesus will "heal every disease."[24] Granted, at the creation this would apply to all human beings, and not just Christians. However, just a few verses later, the group who benefit from Jesus' healing narrows. First, it is Israel who will be transformed by Jesus as "holy daughter Zion" (that is, the nation of Israel) is told to receive her humble, gentle king, "mounted on a foal" who will "undo the godless ordinances and constraining bonds," and "set aside the former, perishable sacrifices." What is Jesus undoing? "Godless ordinances," "constraining bonds," and "sacrifices" are direct references to the Jewish laws of Torah that require, among other things, sacrificing at the Jerusalem temple. So, "holy daughter Zion," through Jesus' arrival, becomes an Israel that has given up traditional Jewish practices and follows Jesus. The author explains, "If Zion" can only "know who he [the humble, gentle king Jesus] is," then she will "see *the begetter*," of a new Zion, a new Israel.[25] Can you hear the echo of the God-of-the-Womb resounding in this passage in its language of begetting, of reproduction? Jesus is now giving birth to Christian sons of God.

Finally, immediately following the detailed description of Jesus' conception in Oracle 8, the author declares, "we are also a holy heavenly race of Christ and are called brethren."[26] Not just sons, but brothers: a new family is emerging. Furthermore, this "race" is clearly demarcated in Oracle 8 from Torah-observant Jews. The group that is disinherited and exiled from God's new family is now Israel itself, specifically, traditional Jews who follow Jewish law and do not recognize Jesus as the Jewish messiah. The birth of a new elect is accomplished.

Conclusion to Part I

We have seen in the biblical texts that conception, gestation, childbirth, and mothering were used to establish the separate and holy identities of Israelites and Christians. The splintering of family ties and the origins of ethnic and national differences in the Bible are central in the mothers' stories. On a very fundamental level, beyond texts, all of this makes perfect sense. As Kristeva described so poetically in the chapter above, the maternal body is precisely where the distinction between self and other is first absent, and then forced into being through childbirth. It is the beginning of difference itself.

The bodily reality of merged being that pregnancy entails, however, presents a very real social and cultural challenge—a point of anxiety—because identity, difference, and relationships originate in and take place only when the fusion of mother and child ends, in childbirth and beyond. As we have seen, mothers have borne the weight of that anxiety, at least since the biblical texts were written.

In my view, this visceral reality feeds not only the stories of the biblical mothers' children becoming enemy nations, but thence (through them and other stories like them) our own ethnic and racial hatreds today. Yet another product of this logic of differentiation is the deeply ambivalent attitudes towards sexuality, especially women's desire, that pervade Western culture, as well as the desexualizing, sanitizing, and idealizing of motherhood. Stereotypes of "good" and "bad" mothers are incredibly resilient, familiar, and fixed in our collective social psyche. They are understood so well they can sometimes make us laugh, and sometimes shake our heads in frustrated protest. Consider the following humorous job description for a mother offered in a 2007 *New York Times* Mother's Day piece:

> Must be exceptionally stable yet ridiculously responsive to the needs of those around you; must be willing to trail after your loved ones, cleaning up their messes and compensating for their deficiencies and selfishness; must work twice as hard as everybody else; must accept blame for a long list of the world's

> illnesses; must have a knack for shaping young minds while in no way neglecting the less glamorous tissues below; must have a high tolerance for babble and repetition; and must agree, when asked, to shut up, fade into the background and pretend you don't exist.[27]

Selflessness, focusing exclusively on others and their needs, moral uprightness, social acceptability, *not* expressing sexuality, preserving home and culture, caring for children: all are still typical expectations of mothers today. These social norms are powerful and deeply moralistic and we have found them in the stories about biblical mothers, just as we do in our culture today.

In the writings that follow in Part II, the mothers that conceive, nourish, and give birth to God's chosen peoples continue to be scrutinized by Jewish and Christian writers over the centuries. In these writings, they are idealized and condemned, lifted up and judged; they are seen as body and spirit, active and passive, virtuous and vulgar. The bodily act of conceiving chosen children becomes more and more a question of the mothers' spiritual righteousness and obedience. In later interpretations of their stories, their sexual and procreative power is regulated, contained, and used by God and the men in their family to their own ends.

In Part II, then, our questions expand. We will use our understanding of early Jewish and Christian ideas about these questions from Part I (as we tried to get there from here) and map the strategic interpretation, adaptation, and transmission of those ideas over time (as we explore how we got here from there).

II

Mansplaining the Mothers

Getting Here from There

INTRODUCTION TO PART II

Before I begin chapter 4, I want to take a minute to present this part of the book as it is framed in my mind. I begin with another recent book and poem, as I have in previous sections. In 1981, coeditors Cherríe Moraga and Gloria Anzaldúa published *This Bridge Called My Back*. It was a collection of personal essays, cultural criticism, interviews, testimonials, poetry, and visual art from the perspective of women of color.[28] A declaration of women of color feminism, their book explored "the complex confluence of identities—race, class, gender, and sexuality—systemic to women-of-color oppression and liberation." It went on to win the 1986 Before Columbus Foundation American Book Award, as well as the 2016 Independent Publisher Book Awards Bronze Medal in the Anthologies category. More importantly, it contributed to the evolution of second-wave feminism to third-wave feminism, challenging prior feminist staples like "universal womanhood" and heteronormativity, by proclaiming the distinct feminist experiences of women of color and lesbians. *This Bridge Called My Back* remains crucial to feminist theorizing to this day.

Here, in the pages below, Part II will be a journey through the ways in which the mothers' stories have been retold, explained, used, and abused in new contexts to buttress a core set of cultural narratives about sexuality, gender, motherhood, and ethnicity. As I move through the continuing uses and abuses of their stories, I hear repeatedly in my mind key lines from Donna Kate Rushin's "Bridge Poem" (published in *This Bridge Called My Back*): "I'm sick of filling in your gaps . . . Find another connection to the rest of the world. Find something else to make you legitimate."

When she wrote her poem, Rushin was talking not just to men, but to white women, heterosexuals, indeed all who constructed her as "Other" in order to establish their own normalcy. In my own mind, Rushin also speaks for Hagar, Tamar, and Ruth—ethnic "Others," all—shouting her lines at Sarah and Abraham, Judah, and Boaz, fists raised.

I cannot help but share the transmission of the mothers' stories over the centuries from Rushin's point of view, the view of the woman who has been made "Other" too long. Through that frame, we may measure the deep relationship between the mothers' stories in the Bible and our own stories about mothers and "Others"—of rivalrous children and rejected branches of family, despised and demeaned groups of people, the disavowing of those who could have been—and should be—held dear. These stories, past and present, weave a web of retellings, made of the same silk, spinning variations of set patterns. In them we can see both historical and current crises of toxic differences. Within the frame of Ruskin's poem, we can do so, refusing to write, or be written into, those patterns anymore.

4

Sarah's Laugh

Sex and the Hebrew Bible Matriarchs

With so many questions left open in the biblical stories, the conversation about the biblical mothers could not but continue across centuries, raising questions no less urgent or impactful. Why does establishing peoplehood and righteousness have to set brother against brother, sister against sister, Israelites against others, Christians against "the world," and maternal power against spiritual obedience? Why does women's power to create life, and the pleasure of doing so, have to be regulated in order to assert a male God's superior life-giving power over wombs, conception, and the creation of "God's" people? Why do these antitheses seem natural, even inevitable to so many?

In this chapter, I will present postbiblical representations of the mothers' sexuality. The relationship between the sexuality of the mothers' bodies and the righteousness of Israel and the Christian church is repeatedly taken up and explored in later writings about the mothers, just as it was in the biblical stories themselves. The question that has persisted over time is whether the mothers' bodies and sexual reproduction were beneficial or dangerous. In the Bible itself, the sexuality of the mothers is clearly a theme—from Sarah to Mary—and in later writings their sexual and reproductive acts are examined, judged, shamed, and applauded over and over again, whether it be Lot's daughters, Tamar, Ruth, or Mary.

Even more than the sexually transgressive mothers who followed her, Sarah has been the target of extensive attention by Jewish and Christian writers, perhaps matched only by Eve, the mother of all humanity, and Mary, the mother of Jesus. As the first mother of Israel, Sarah has received some positive spin. As we shall see in chapter 6, her righteousness has been asserted and celebrated by some writers. Predictably, these texts closely resemble expectations of moral integrity in mothers today. Sarah has been praised as an ideal wife, even a prophetess, who enjoyed a close relationship with God, engaging in prayer with God at key moments in her biography. At the same time, Sarah has been depicted as blind to God's power, hopelessly focused on her body, and ignorant of spiritual truths. Her idealization or condemnation depends on whether her spiritual and social righteousness is the topic, or her body and its pleasure. A good example of this logic can be found in later interpretations of Sarah's laugh when angels announce that she will conceive in Genesis 18. Sarah's body-focused responses to their message are presented as antithetical to moral and spiritual righteousness. Let's review the details of that annunciation in more detail.

When the angels of God come to Abraham's tent at Mamre to announce that Sarah will conceive post-menopause, Sarah has a striking reaction. At that moment Sarah does not marvel at God's power, but instead laughs at the biological impossibility of the Lord's promise. She reacts based on her knowledge of her own body.

In case Sarah's reaction seems like a small thing, it may help to remember that there are many such scenes in the Hebrew Bible when angels announce to infertile women that the God-of-the-Womb will give them a favored son. None of them laugh! Manoah's wife, who is the mother of Samson; Hannah, the mother of the prophet Samuel; and Hagar, the mother of Ishmael all trust in God's power and obey God's commands regarding their children without delay. Yet awe and obedience do not characterize Sarah's response to God's intervention.[29] Sarah's laugh is different. In fact, the angel who speaks to the couple draws attention to this, asking why she laughed. She lies and says she did not. Sarah's lie suggests that she feels shame or fear about laughing. This is reinforced when the angel holds her accountable: "Yes, you did laugh."

As if all this were not enough, there is an additional dimension to Sarah's laugh that sexualizes her response, for the Hebrew word used to describe Sarah's laugh also has a sexual meaning. In the Hebrew Bible, it means "to play or sport," often referring to sexual arousal. This suggests that Sarah is also laughing at the idea of her postmenopausal body experiencing sexual pleasure. This is very interesting since a woman achieving orgasm was understood in some ancient medical treatises to ensure conception. Perhaps Sarah equates conception with orgasm!

Sarah's focus on both the impossibility of, and the importance of having an orgasm to, her conceiving is not unheard of in her culture. Yet, the angel's reaction suggests something very different. It asserts that she is blind to God's power to control human conception, blind to his ability to miraculously make her conceive. The angel asks, "Is anything too hard for the Lord?" With this rhetorical question, God's decisive role in producing the child of the promise, and thereby the nation of Israel, is asserted, while Sarah's role in sexual reproduction and conception—much less sexual pleasure—is made irrelevant. Certainly, her barrenness and menopause are insignificant.

The separation of sexual pleasure and righteous maternity is implied; this message has certainly persisted over time. Righteous conception of righteous children is the only goal, *not* sexual pleasure. Sarah's reaction is presented as a problem. What is interesting to me is that she seems to know this when she quickly denies laughing. A real tension is created throughout this scene. Sarah's central status as *righteous* mother of chosen descendants is contrasted with her apparent continuing disrespect for God. She does not see that the (pro)creation of Israel is a divine, not a human, process. She continues to misunderstand this, just as she did in Genesis 16 when she tried to use Hagar to produce the promised child.

In Genesis 21, the follow-up and resolution to the promise at Mamre, God intervenes and opens Sarah's womb, transforming her early attempts to produce a righteous human seed through Abraham and Hagar, into a divine seed, consecrated and set apart by God himself. If the righteousness of Israel is often linked to the sister-wife, the ultimate fertility that produces it must come directly from God. Sarah's sexually charged laugh is the very opposite of this message.

From this small story line, Sarah's laugh became a point of reference for later Jewish writers to work through the role of female sexuality and the maternal body in creating Israel. A particularly influential commentary on Sarah's laugh was written by a rabbi-scholar named Rashi, who lived in France in the eleventh century. He is often called the father of all commentators because his writings are still, to this day, considered indispensable to the study of the Hebrew Bible. In his reading of Sarah's laugh, Rashi roundly denies and rewrites Sarah's playful reference to her own sexual pleasure, explaining that she is not talking about pleasure at all, but rather only asking about her biological capacity to perform procreative functions. Rashi writes, "She looked at her insides and said, 'Is it possible that these insides can carry a child, these shriveled breasts can draw milk?'"[30] Thus Rashi erases Sarah's passion. In this way, her righteousness is somewhat salvaged. She is not expressing inappropriate (in rabbinic eyes) interest in her own sexual pleasure. She is focusing on procreation. Sarah may misunderstand God's power to control the female reproductive system, but at least she understands her procreative obligations and limitations.

About a hundred years later, another French rabbi and biblical commentator, Radak, finds greater fault in Sarah. He takes Sarah's laugh as much more than questions about her body; instead, Sarah is the epitome of flawed human understanding, including ignorance about her own infertility. She understands nothing, not even that "the man who had made the prediction was an angel . . ." Her laugh is "derisive," though she has enough "good manners" to not "laugh in the angel's face." Radak concludes that the angel has nothing but disdain for Sarah:

> Even though the angel did not answer her point by point, he did answer her with an overall statement that there simply is nothing which is beyond God's power to accomplish if he so desires . . . The angel did not even bother to reply to Sarah's statement that her husband was too old to impregnate her with semen. The reason he did not do so was that Sarah having had her menopause was the far greater natural impediment to her becoming pregnant. It is not altogether unknown for old men to father children even in their advanced old age.[31]

Not only is Sarah's body a problem, Radak now makes her a symbol of "the [inadequate] eyes of human beings that cannot fathom how such things can be . . . In light of God's omnipotence, nothing is impossible for Him to accomplish. He who created the universe has no problem making changes in His universe [e.g., in women's wombs]."[32]

Radak's reading is typical of many interpretations that have focused on Sarah's ignorance. Often, they stress the superiority of Abraham's knowledge (over Sarah's) and demonstrate this through their respective responses to God's announcement. They argue that Abraham recognized the angels as angels, while Sarah did not. Not only has Radak erased the audacity of Sarah's sexual response, not only is her maternal power irrelevant compared to God's power, but her spiritual understanding and knowledge are negative examples for all of humanity. Here again, the lesson is that the mother must be asexual, recognize God's power over her, and be a spiritual and moral example, or pay the price of judgement.

As should be clear by now, however, judgements of the mothers are never final, in the Hebrew Bible or in later writings. They build and feed on one another, creating the web of maternal stereotypes and expectations mothers still face today. Certainly, the primary question is always all about the child—is the child from God, chosen, righteous? Yet, the mother's body cannot be excised from the answer to that question. Thus, ongoing anxiety about Sarah's body and sexual actions, and the mystery of her conception of Isaac, continued.

One way that this anxiety is expressed is through questions of paternity, which raise the possibility that Sarah is promiscuous. A persistent discomfort with Abraham's apparently passive role in conceiving his son persists, specifically whether that could signal an illicit conception. This anxiety surfaces in a particularly interesting story told by Rashi about "scoffers" who doubted Abraham's paternity. The story goes as follows:

> *Abraham was the father of Isaac*. . . . It became necessary to say, "Abraham was the father of Isaac," because the scoffers of the generations were saying that Sarah conceived by Abimelech, for she had lived with Abraham many years and did not conceive by him. What did God do? He shaped Isaac's facial features similar to Abraham's so that everyone would testify that "Abraham was the father of Isaac." This is [the meaning of] what is written here: "Isaac, son of Abraham" for here is proof that "Abraham was Isaac's father."[33]

The possibility that Abraham was not Isaac's biological father—refuted in the story by God's reshaping of Isaac's features—is as much about Sarah's sexual virtue (was she impregnated by King Abimelech while in his custody earlier?) as it is about the chosenness of her son. I would further note that an intervention by God that changes the shape of Isaac's face is not exactly "proof" that Abraham is the father. It seems to me to prove that God is the one who shapes Isaac to his own purposes, before and after his birth. This is also a strange defense against potential misunderstandings of Sarah's virtue in the community. It does not really answer the question of whether Sarah conceived without the help of her husband.

I'll offer one more rabbinic interpretation that reveals questions and tensions about Sarah's—and Abraham's—sexual and procreative bodies. This passage also continues to drive home the overarching primary message that God, not human beings, is the ultimate father of Israel. This text, *Yevamot,* comes from an early collection of rabbinic writings called the *Mishnah* in the section on women and marriage. It was written down around 200 CE.

Before I begin the story, it may help to point out that passages in the *Mishnah* have a particular format. Knowing what it is will make the meaning of the passage below clearer. The format is the texts record different rabbis having a conversation together about a particular question. They begin with a biblical verse that they wish to explain. A rabbi will begin, making a point about the Bible verse. He will usually quote and interpret additional biblical verses to back up his point. Then other rabbis will comment on his point and those verses, sometimes adding other biblical verses of their own to develop or contradict what has been said. Such is the following passage which seeks to explain Isaiah 51:1–2 (included in the quotation). Along the way, the discussion literally unsexes Abraham and Sarah at a fundamental, physical level:

> Rabbi Ami said: Abraham and Sarah were originally *tumtumin*, people whose sexual organs are concealed and not functional, as it is stated: "Look to the rock from where you were hewn, and to the hole of the pit from where you were dug" (Isaiah 51:1), and it is written in the next verse: "Look to Abraham your father and to Sarah who bore you" (Isaiah 51:2), which indicates that sexual organs were fashioned for them, signified by the words hewn and dug, over the course of time. Rav Na⊠man said that Rabba bar Avuh said: Our mother Sarah was initially a sexually underdeveloped woman [*aylonit*], as it is stated: "And Sarah was barren; she had no child" (*Genesis* 11:30). The superfluous words: "She had no child," indicate that she did not have even a place, i.e., a womb, for a child.[34]

This story of God creating the reproductive organs of Sarah and Abraham (her "hole/pit" and his "rock") is fascinating because it directly follows a series of stern reminders by the rabbis of the punishments for anyone in Israel who does *not* procreate. Anyone who does not engage in the command to be fruitful and multiply is a murderer, they say, a threat to God's image, and those who refuse will cause God to withdraw from all of Israel entirely.

The inclusion of a patriarch, and not just a matriarch, in this explanation of God-given, and God-approved, procreative equipment is powerful in light of such an ominous imperative. Other rabbinic texts also pursue this theme of God-given patriarchal virility, but from another angle. They insist on a kind of precocious hyper-fertility in the patriarchs as children. Like rabbinic writings that elsewhere establish Abraham's virility in old age at the time Isaac was conceived, these texts provide assurances about patriarchal procreative capacity in early childhood. For example, the *Mishnah*[35] claims that, "in earlier generations men fathered children at the age of eight." Rabbi Yitzhak cites Genesis 17:17 where Abraham specifies that he is one hundred years old, and Sarah ninety years old at the time God announces Isaac's imminent birth. From that passage, R. Yitzhak reasons that Sarah's father, Haran, "begot" her at the age of eight as follows: "How much older was Abraham than Sarah? He was ten years older than her and, as stated above, he was two years older than her father, Haran. It turns out then that when Haran begot Sarah, he begot her at the age of eight."

Take note that these claims about patriarchal virility do not function in the same way that the never-ending questioning of the matriarchs does. Quite the opposite, in fact. Such rabbinic passages decisively put to rest any questioning of the patriarchs' ability to produce chosen descendants. As I've suggested above, God's role in "opening the wombs" of the matriarchs may have necessitated such claims to patriarchal hyper-fertility, to counterbalance their apparent absence from the procreative process. This does not change the fact that their procreative ability is repeatedly defended, while the mothers continually remain on trial.

JUST HOW SEXY ARE THE MOTHERS' BED-TRICKS?

Many later writings focus on the physical, bodily processes that empowered the mothers to conceive chosen sons in unlikely circumstances, from Lot's daughters in the cave to Mary and the angel at the annunciation. The question of whether and how they might be sexual or spiritual is central. This question is approached through surprisingly detailed dissections of how maternal bodies created the chosen, saved, and disavowed. The end result has been the desexualizing of the mothers' conceptions and the establishment of God's control over their bodies. Only in this way can the unique righteousness of the patriarchs and their sons be assured.

We have seen that the mothers, especially the Davidic mothers, took unconventional, aggressive control of the procreation of their sons. Lot's daughters, Tamar, and Ruth all tricked or seduced the fathers of their sons into having sex with them. Later interpreters of their stories are left with many pressing questions as a result, and all are focused on sexuality and spirituality.

Questions abound about Lot's daughters, for instance, in later Jewish writings. Did they really believe there were no more men on the earth? Were they really virgins? How did they become pregnant on the first try? Are Lot's daughters sexually immoral wannabe-mothers who must be kept at arm's length? Deliberations on these questions can get pretty technical.

Did they really believe there were no more men in the world? According to several respected rabbinic texts,[36] including the fourteenth century *Rabbeinu Bachya*,[37] the answer is yes. The relevant passage argues as follows:

> Our sages . . . give these daughters credit for having wanted to preserve the human species as they thought they and their father were the sole survivors during that generation. Seeing that their mother had died during the flight from Sodom, their father was left without a mate and had no other chance of perpetuating the

> human species unless his daughters would give birth to a male child by being impregnated by him. This is why they went on record with the words: "There is no other man on earth to have intercourse with us" (verse 31) in order to justify what would otherwise appear as frivolous conduct. This is why the Torah refrained from using any expression criticizing their conduct as incestuous or licentious. Their intentions were absolutely pure.

Here we have "absolutely pure" spiritual foremothers who prioritized the continuation of the human race above their own sexual purity, thus exemplifying spiritual purity.

On the other hand, the answer is a definitive no, according to our old friend Radak (no friend to the mothers, as we saw with Sarah), as well as the later thirteenth-century *Tur HaArokh*.[38] These texts instead argue that the daughters did not think the destruction and death of all men was worldwide, but rather feared that having survived Sodom, they would be seen as wicked, and no men would want to marry them.[39] Even more interesting, a further specific reference to *genetic* defects is made in *Tur HaArokh*: "They assumed that such men would feel they had been *genetically harmed* so that they could not bear healthy children, if at all."

Is this not the very opposite of the genealogical righteousness ascribed to all who transmit the divinely chosen Abrahamic seed? On the other hand, any inappropriate sexual desire is also decidedly absent from these texts. This is often what we find in the rabbinic presentations of the incestuous encounter between Lot's daughters and their father. They downplay sexuality and foreground spiritual outcomes. In doing this, they recuperate and vindicate the daughters, desexualize the incest, and affirm a God-facilitated, righteous working through of God's plans for Israel's future. Let's look at a few more examples.

Another question that worried later Jewish writers is how the daughters became pregnant on their first night of ever having sex, since ancient medical and gynecological texts asserted that this was not possible. In order to explain this contradiction, Rashi repeats an answer found in an earlier rabbinic text, *Genesis Rabbah*, which explained that the daughters *broke their own hymens* so that they would get pregnant in one night. This is decidedly unsexual; in fact, it is usually a painful procedure, the opposite of pleasure. The breaking of their hymens is a sacrifice the daughters make for the good of the human race.

In addition, Rashi goes on to explain that the wine that made Lot drunk was already in the cave when Lot and his daughters arrived there, "[so] that they might bring forth two nations."[40] Thus Bachya ben Asher (thirteenth century) also explains and expands, "The sages say that Lot's daughters enjoyed a divine assist in their undertaking. The wine itself was found in their cave. They had not brought it with them. God had provided it to make their undertaking easier."[41]

These details are also noted by many additional commentators. In all cases, they serve to exonerate the daughters. The rationale is that righteous offspring, essential to the continuance of Israel, would come into being through the daughters' incest. God's motive in supplying wine in the cave is to enable the procreative process that would ultimately result in the birth of King David.

Consequently, in *Tur HaArokh*, the older daughter is said to be rewarded by God for initiating the procreative process. Her reward is that her descendant is Ruth, the virtuous and loyal Moabite who would give birth to Obed, the grandfather of the great Israelite king, David. We may also note that in the Christian tradition, this makes her a foremother of the Christian savior, Jesus of Nazareth:

> The sages say that the older daughter who initiated sleeping with her father a single night before her sister was rewarded by God in that from her issue Ruth joined the Jewish people, whereas Naamah from Ammon who became the wife of Rechavam [Rehoboam], son of Solomon, did not join the Jewish people until four generations later.[42]

This and related readings demonstrate a validating of the daughters' incest, now completely desexualized and reinterpreted as faithful obedience to God's long-term genealogical plans for Israel.[43] Importantly, these are not simply later medieval revisions of early Jewish thinking. The transformation of the daughters' sexual transgressions into fulfilling the will of God can be traced all the way back to the second-century *Mishnah* in the following passage:

> And with regard to the daughters of Lot, Rabbi ☒iyya bar Abba says that Rabbi Yehoshua ben Kor☒a says: A person should always hasten to perform a mitzva [commandment], as due to the one night by which the elder daughter of Lot preceded the younger daughter, with the intention of performing a mitzva [be fruitful and multiply] by bringing children into the world, she preceded her by four generations in having her descendants enter into the Jewish people. They are: Obed, son of Ruth the Moabite, Yishai, David, and Solomon. Whereas, the descendants of the younger daughter did not join the Jewish people until Rehoboam, Solomon's son, was born, as it is written: "And his mother's name was Naamah the Ammonite."

This desexualizing and spiritual recuperation of Lot's daughters reinforces the overarching theme of the procreative action of God himself on the mothers' wombs. Indeed, God's direct action on the daughters is made even more explicit in another rabbinic text, *Genesis Rabbah*, in which Rabbi Tanhuma interprets the daughters' impregnations as directly from God:

> "Come, let us make our father drink wine, and we will lie with him, that we may preserve offspring through our father" (Genesis 19:32). Rabbi Tanhuma said in Samuel's name: It is not written that we may preserve a child of our father, but "that we may preserve offspring (seed) *through* our Father": namely the seed that comes from another place [from heaven]—and this is the messiah.[44]

By this interpretation, it is "a seed from another place," God's seed, that impregnates the daughters. The name given by the first daughter to her son, Moab, "son of my father," now refers to God, the Father, and the "messiah," King David, is the son of God.[45] This argument is an interesting mix of the Hebrew Bible focus on a God who opens wombs and the intensely spiritualizing efforts of the medieval interpretations above.

All these examples demonstrate how rabbinic discussions of the Hebrew Bible constantly expand and build on each other. Like the Bible itself, the rabbinic writings are a conversation. When it comes to the mothers, that conversation is never finished. The medieval texts I've cited above illustrate one set of interpretations of Lot's daughters. They attempt to redeem and sanitize their incest. There are, however, opposing traditions. Rashi, for instance, does not ascribe spiritual motives to Lot's daughters. He describes the daughter's incest as sexual, labeling it "unchaste conduct," "sin," and "their shame."[46] As for Lot, Rashi quotes from the *Mishnah*: "R. Levi said, 'Whoever is inflamed by sexual desire will, in the end, be made to eat his own flesh.'"[47]

In a similar vein, Radak also judges Lot's daughters harshly, yet he also chooses to defend Lot's righteousness. According to Radak, Lot is completely unaware of his actions, while the daughters perform "such a despicable act."

> He certainly would not agree to sleep with his daughters while in full possession of his faculties. Anyone subscribing to the cultural mores of an Abraham would not knowingly engage in such a practice. This story is related in order to teach us that even people not subscribing to the moral standards of the Torah would not stoop to this kind of sexual licentiousness. The entire story reveals the origin of the peoples of Ammon and Moab . . . Lot would have resisted the sexual union with his daughter and

> would have severely remonstrated with her for performing such a despicable act.[48]

Radak moves explicitly to a focus on sexuality and sexual desire. He denies that Lot felt any desire or would condone anything that happened in the cave, while attributing to the daughters "sexual licentiousness." The rejection of incest in "the culture of Abraham" is emphatically affirmed. I also cannot help but note here that Radak assumes sexual pleasure ("licentiousness") in young virginal girls having sex with their father, a concept with a violent and damaging legacy in our culture. It's easy to get lost in the historical and cultural agendas of texts and unconsciously absorb without defense the incredibly destructive messages beneath the rhetoric. It is only later, on a second or third reading, that readers may stop and feel the transhistorical power of our stories about women. Young virginal girls do not have pleasure while having sex with their fathers.

Once felt, this will permeate readers' responses to all related texts. For example, turning again to *Tur HaArokh*, we find the argument that in Jewish law (Torah), "it was permissible for a father to have sexual relations with his daughter."[49] The text, however, immediately counters that legal interpretation, explaining that while,

> there was no legal impediment to their father marrying them, it had become a universally accepted norm after the deluge that fathers would not touch their daughters, sexually. The matter is discussed in *Horiyot,* where deviates were described as being guilty of committing an abomination.[50]

This argument describes an evolution of cultural standards that move beyond prior laws. It resembles other Talmudic[51] texts, such as *Sanhedrin* 58b.7–11, for example, which debates reasons why Adam did not marry his daughter. Was it because it was not permissible, or was it because he wanted Cain to marry her? Is it all right for men to marry their sisters? *When did it stop being permissible?*

> At the beginning of the world's existence it was permitted for men to marry their sisters, which was later forbidden in the verse: "And if a man shall take his sister . . . it is a shameful thing" (*Leviticus* 20:17). The Gemara [later rabbinic commentary] infers: If it had not been so, if God had not specially permitted Cain to marry his sister, she would have been forbidden to him.

Here it is the law that corrects the cultural standard, not vice versa. The text of *Sanhedrin* was being collected in the fifth to sixth centuries. Clearly, the biblical incest stories were still being worked through many centuries after they were first written down. Lot's daughters find themselves in the crosshairs of that endeavor; the possibility that they (or their father) felt sexual pleasure is an abiding fear that persists. Thus, the daughters' sexual and spiritual virtue continues to be evaluated. Within this ongoing interpretive negotiation, qualifications, justifications, condemnations, denials, and idealizations compete for lasting cultural influence.

Before we leave Lot's daughters and move on to other sexually aggressive/transgressive mothers, let's ride the pendulum one more time back towards a spiritual reading of a daughter of Lot. This daughter, however, was not in the cave; thus, the author sidesteps questions of sexuality and procreation entirely. That's one way to solve the problem of biblical women's sexuality and reaffirm a virtuous Abrahamic seed running through Lot's lineage.

This reading of Lot's third daughter first appears in the second-century *Mishnah*, though not specifically identifying the young heroine as Lot's daughter. It then shows up in a medieval work of the eighth century, *Pirke Rabbi Eliezer.* Later, it resurfaces in a fourteenth-century popular ethical work from Spain, entitled *Sefer HaYashar*. Notice how the web of interpretations is woven over time.

In the earliest *Mishnah* version, the story begins in Sodom, before the angels destroy the city. I will point out before you read the passage that the young woman conceals her acts of charity from the people of Sodom because they were known to mistreat the poor, travelers, or anyone needing assistance. (Remember how they treated the poor visiting angels in Lot's house!) The Sodomites were known, first and foremost, for their lack of hospitality. Not so our heroine. The *Mishnah* version reads as follows:

> There was a young woman who would take bread out to the poor people in a pitcher so the people of Sodom would not see it. The matter was revealed, and they smeared her with honey and positioned her on the wall of the city, and the hornets came and consumed her. And that is the meaning of that which is written: "And the Lord said: Because the cry of Sodom and Gomorrah is great" (*Genesis* 18:20). And Rav Yehuda says that Rav says: "Great" is an allusion to the matter of the young woman who was killed for her act of kindness. It is due to that sin that the fate of the people of Sodom was sealed.[52]

In the eighth century, *Pirke Rabbi Eliezer* picks up the story, but identifies the young woman as a daughter of Lot named Peletith. She is married to a rich man of Sodom. In spite of the proclamation stating that anyone who helps the poor will be burned to death, Peletith feeds a poor man every day, secretly, until she is discovered. As they take her to the fire, she cries out to God:

> "Sovereign of all worlds! Maintain my right and my cause (at the hands of) the men of Sodom." And her cry ascended before the Throne of Glory. In that hour the Holy One, blessed be He, said: "I will now descend, and I will see (Gen. 18:21) whether the men of Sodom have done according to the cry of this young woman."[53]

This story serves to distinguish the family of Lot from the Sodomites, through the appearance of an additional daughter who exhibits Abrahamic righteousness and hospitality. Finally, the story is repeated in *Sefer HaYashar* twice, first in a story about Peletith, who dies by fire in Sodom, and secondly, in a parallel narrative about a maiden in the town of Admah, who is anointed with honey and placed near a hive of bees (more explicitly linking the story back to the *Sanhedrin* passage). It is in the second narrative that the maiden's "cries of agony" reach heaven and enrage God, prompting him to send the angels to destroy Sodom.[54]

In terms of how stories function, it is essential that we note the dire escalation of the consequences that await condemned "Others" in these stories. In these stories of Peletith, the righteousness of an Abrahamic woman serves not just to differentiate the chosen family from sinful "Others" (the Sodomites). It also explicitly brings about the divine annihilation of the Sodomite Others. This plot detail also has a legacy. Calling down God's judgement in a firestorm is not an unheard-of rhetorical move today when Christians speak of sinful "Others." It is a dangerous logic that is demonstrated over and over again in the biblical texts.

That is to say, these stories about the mothers and daughters are incredibly resilient, as they are told and retold from the second to the fourteenth century, ranging from Palestine to Spain. Their messages have had wide-ranging and persistent influence on cultural ideals of what women should be, and what "Others" deserve. In the context of this chapter specifically, the condemnation of the mothers' sexual pleasure and the promotion of their spiritual selflessness, martyrdom, and mothering of virtuous men endure through these traditions.[55]

VIRGIN MATRIARCHS AND THEIR NOT-SO-PRIVATE PARTS

We return in this section to Rashi's eleventh-century claim that Lot's daughters *broke their own hymens* so that they would become pregnant during their first intercourse, a feat that would otherwise have been seen as impossible physiologically. I have indicated that rabbinic explanations for the matriarchs' conceptions can get technical, as technical as the descriptions of conception in the second-century Christian texts we looked at in chapter 3. In this section, this will be amply demonstrated. It turns out that the fixation on the matriarchs' deflowering of themselves is repeated over time across rabbinic interpretations, most predominantly in medieval rabbinic writings. Modern scholars' responses to these accounts are interesting. They include seeing the mothers' self-defloration as empowering for them since it gives them control over the conception of their children. Other scholars today argue that these male authors continued to feel the need to produce stories that established the mothers' sexual purity. As for ordinary women readers, they may have an unhappy reading experience in the next section as they are confronted with the voyeuristic male gaze in these texts that scrutinizes the mothers' intimate parts with such a sense of license and ownership.

The theme of digital defloration ("crushing with the finger") does not appear in the Hebrew Bible, nor in any Jewish texts until roughly 200–600 CE, when additional commentaries on the *Mishnah* were written (known as *gemara*).[56] Two external pressures weighed on these later commentators and may have been responsible for the introduction and resilience of this motif. Both are linked to the way defloration effectively established the virginity (sexual virtue) of the matriarchs. First, they were responding to the inherited and ever-renewing tradition of concern about the "inappropriate" sexuality of the matriarchs (discussed above). A second pressure, however, was also at work: the impact on rabbinic writers of the powerful Christian story of the virginity of Jesus' mother, Mary.

Regarding the first pressure, we have looked so far at rabbinic writings in order to explore how they judged the matriarchs' spiritual and sexual righteousness. There were, however, many non-rabbinic Jewish writings—such as *Jubilees*—that also retold the mothers' stories, in the context of their own cultural questions and concerns. Some examples of these will be included below to make clear that the rabbis were not the only judges of the mothers; they were instead part of a larger cultural conversation about them.

The second pressure, that of the virginity of Jesus' mother, Mary, also reminds us of the importance of cultural and literary context. Biblical interpreters always combine their readings of an original text with preceding interpretations of it, *but also in response to their particular historical, cultural, and literary worlds.* This becomes more and more relevant as one moves through the ever-evolving history of interpretations, *because* cultural and literary contexts change as time passes. Christianity began as a sect of traditional Judaism and the slow separation of these two forms of Judaism meant that closely related yet dueling narratives of the mothers began to appear.[57] Up to this point, I have been presenting ways in which the matriarchs' stories informed later narratives about the Virgin Mary. However, as the web of interpretations of the mothers evolved over time, influence began to move in both directions. Mary's virginity was a central belief in the emerging Christian tradition and so, at the same time, the matriarchs' virginity received renewed attention in Hebrew Bible commentaries. A good example of this can be found in rabbinic accounts of the mothers' breaking of their own hymens. Looking in both directions, we will also explore Christian parallel texts and early church fathers' fixation on Mary's intact hymen in the next chapter.

Rabbinic commentaries that feature self-defloration include discussions of the matriarchs Hagar, Lot's daughters, Rebecca, and Tamar.[58] The first mention of a mother deflowering herself appears in the fifth-century *Genesis Rabbah*. Preceding (and perhaps provoking) this first rabbinic mention, however, were prior texts that judged the mothers' sexuality. Let's look at a particularly negative presentation of Tamar from the second century BCE *Testament of Judah*. *Testament of Judah* is part of a collection of final testaments. These feature the final words of each of the twelve sons of Jacob to their families. There are thus twelve testaments. In them, the patriarchs review their lives and offer moral exhortations to their descendants based on their experiences. All demonstrate a deeply misogynistic outlook, filled with repeated warnings about the terrifying power and sexual threat that women represent for men.

In *Testament of Judah*, Judah's marriage to the Canaanite Shua and the family they created together is transformed into a story of drunken lust, curses, and death. In it, Shua is the mother who is problematic and meddling. She insists that her sons, Er and Onan, *not* have intercourse with Tamar, *because she is not Canaanite*.[59] Shua's prohibition of her sons' procreative acts accomplishes both the demonization of Judah's Canaanite wife and the elevation of Tamar as (at least) not a hated Canaanite. Both sons die for their anti-procreative actions, yet the hatred of Canaanites is sustained. Consider this speech by Judah:

> And I knew that the race of the Canaanites was evil, but youthful impulses blinded my reason, and when I saw her [Shua, his wife], I was led astray by the strong drink and had intercourse with her. While I was absent, she went off and brought from Canaan a wife for Shelah [their third son]. When I realized what she had done, I pronounced a curse on her in the anguish of my soul, and she died in her wickedness, together with her children.[60] (Luke 1:31–33)

Particularly relevant to questions of maternal sexuality is the claim in *Testament of Judah* that Tamar was, in fact, a whore. The author sets this claim up as follows. He makes clear that Tamar is not a Canaanite, but she is also not Israelite. Instead, she is identified as an Amorite, from Mesopotamia. Then, in the scene where Tamar seduces Judah on the street, the author explains, "There is a law among the Amorites that a woman who was widowed should sit in public like a whore."[61] The bed-trick has become a reality in *Testament of Judah*. Furthermore, while Judah does express guilt and repentance in this story, he also continues to distrust and blame Tamar, referring to the way she "tricked herself out" as a prostitute, how he was drunk and didn't know what he was doing (sound like Lot?), and even asking himself, "What if she did it deceitfully, having received my things from some other woman?" The combination of ethnic and gender denunciation and abasement here is not pretty. With these themes in mind, we can now return to the fifth-century *Genesis Rabbah* and its first mention of a mother deflowering herself.

The discussion of defloration begins with a rabbi asking how Hagar conceived on her first night with Abraham (understood as impossible, as we've established). The argument is made that Lot's daughters conceived on their first intercourse with a man, so why not Hagar? At this point, Rabbi Tanhuma makes the now familiar claim that Lot's daughters broke their hymens so that it would be possible to conceive. So far, we have simply found the first text that floats this solution. However, this text also provides a clue as to how self-defloration was evaluated by at least one rabbi. Right after the daughters' self-defloration is established, Rabbi Chanina ben Pazi says: "Thorns are neither weeded nor sown, but they grow and spring up on their own. But how much suffering and effort for wheat to grow!"[62]

This metaphor equates "thorns" with ordinary offspring who are easily brought into the world, while "wheat," which symbolizes the chosen children of the matriarchs, requires maternal suffering and difficult effort. For Rabbi Chanina, when Lot's daughters break their own hymens, they are accepting the suffering and hard work necessary to produce God's chosen. This is a very positive reading of their reproductive actions.

As we move into medieval retellings of matriarchal self-deflorations, however, the initial concern about physical impediments to conception, such as hymens, gives way once again to core questions of maternal sexual desire and paternal control of the maternal body. For instance, in a twelfth-century anthology of rabbinic writings entitled *Sekhel Tov*, a discussion that links Hagar's conception to those of Lot's daughters is again offered. The question is once again how Hagar and Lot's daughters conceived in one night, but in this text the rabbis introduce a new claim. Rabbi Levi ben Heyata explains that during first intercourse, the hymen does not open in modest maidens, but only in promiscuous ones, such as Lot's daughters.[63]

This is a strange idea to introduce: if Lot's daughters are promiscuous and their hymens would open in any case, why would they need to break their own hymens? And what does this say about Hagar? She too conceived on the first try with Abraham. Is she also promiscuous? An anatomical question has become a sexual-moral question in this text. The sexual virtue of the mothers is again front and center, but is this really surprising? Male anxiety about the mothers' sexual desire is persistent if nothing else. In these medieval texts, there is little consensus. Do the mothers suffer to produce the chosen, or are they promiscuously enjoying themselves as they commit incest with their father? Hebrew Bible scholar David Malkiel refers to this ambiguity as "the theme of promiscuous virgins or virtuous harlots."[64] We find it again in yet another medieval rabbinic text, the fourteenth-century *Midrash HaGadol*, written in Yemen. This time the matriarch Tamar is the mother in question.

The passage in *Midrash HaGadol* that introduces Tamar into the deliberations about matriarchal self-defloration bases itself in an earlier rabbinic text, *Yevamot* (part of the *Mishnah*), written about eight centuries before *Sekhel Tov*. The *Yevamot* passage repeats the tradition that Lot's daughters deflowered themselves and then reads as follows: "And thus, too, did Tamar control herself, and crush and remove her virginity, and she was impregnated from Judah's penetration, which was her second."[65]

So did Tamar prepare her body before she presented herself as a prostitute to her father-in-law in order to trick her way back into his family. Thus, she became the foremother of King David, just as Lot's daughters before her. Surely the Davidic mothers appear more virtuous through these rabbinic interpretations, their bed-trickery counteracted by their virginal status, spiritual purity, and procreative achievements. This amounts to an effective counter-narrative to *Testament of Judah*'s depiction of Tamar.

At the same time, some problematic questions about Tamar remained that needed to be dealt with, for she had been married twice to Judah's sons, Er and Onan. How could she have been a virgin then? The answer from the rabbis is that Er and Onan had sex with Tamar "unnaturally," a euphemism that refers to anal intercourse.[66] Given the tenor of the original story of Tamar in Genesis 38, these unnatural and non-procreative acts could be lain at the feet of Er and Onan, procreative slackers that they were. Tamar, on the other hand, is wronged on multiple counts. Thus, she becomes eminently recuperable, in spite of her sexual bed-trickery.

If the rabbis thus extend the practice of self-defloration backward in time to Hagar, and thence through Lot's daughters to Tamar in this version, they also extend it forward to women of their own second century, as follows: "Surely Tamar conceived from a first contact! The other answered him:

Tamar crushed with her finger; for Rabbi Isaac said: *All women of the house of Rabbi* who crushed [the hymen] with their finger are called 'Tamar.' And why are they called Tamar? Because Tamar crushed with her finger."[67]

So, who are these "women of the house of Rabbi"? Here, the term "Rabbi" is used as the proper name for Judah the Prince, a revered rabbi who collected all prior rabbinic discussions into the second-century *Mishnah.* The women in Judah's house thus belonged to a highly respected ruling family. They attributed to themselves Davidic lineage and according to this medieval reading, imitated their foremother, Tamar, taking sexual matters into their own hands to ensure that they bore Davidic children. They even took her name to make these connections more visible.

Whether this account reflects a historical reality or merely rabbinic fantasies of maternal obedience is difficult to say. In fact, many interpretations of these claims are possible. Hebrew Bible scholar Kara-Ivanov Kaniel offers several readings.[68] She suggests that the women could have been deflowering themselves to make tests of their virginity impossible, implying sexual promiscuity or resistant sexual autonomy. They could have been victims of an oppressive custom that forced them into conception as quickly as possible. As interesting as these questions are, they are historical in nature. In this book, we are concerned with the legacy of stories about the sexuality of biblical mothers, that is, the messages about maternal sexuality that have been transmitted through them over time.

What we see here, then, is that the rabbis continued to celebrate, even promote, the sexually autonomous act of self-defloration, but only in order to hasten the conception of the chosen. In these texts, the ends are presented as justifying the means. While I have suggested that their claims were in part responses to earlier Jewish retellings of the mothers' stories, such as *Testament of Judah,* they should also be understood in the context of emerging Mariological themes and doctrines, and the popularity of Mary in Christian communities. Christian texts celebrating Mary's virginity and intact hymen developed predominantly from the second to the fifth centuries, making them contemporary to many of the Jewish texts examined above. That parallel tradition, to which we now turn, will lead us further along in understanding how mothers were understood to define peoples.

5

Theotokos, "Mother of God"

The Virgin Mary and Her Miraculous Hymen

MARY, THE MOTHERS, AND HUMAN SALVATION

As I've argued all along, Mary should be seen as the last in the line of Israelite mothers. Like them, she functions to legitimate her son and her religious community as chosen, saved, and distinct from all other groups. In Mary's case, however, the scrutiny she undergoes regarding her family status, contained sexuality, and moral righteousness is intensified and amplified to near breaking point. As always it will be important to recognize the diversity of claims and explanations within these traditions. Like the Jewish texts analyzed in chapter 4, the Christian texts in this chapter are extremely wide-ranging, written between the second and the eighth centuries CE and originating in Palestine, Syria, North Africa, Egypt, Italy, and France. Scholars have traditionally divided early Christian biblical commentary into Eastern and Western traditions. Eastern Christianity celebrated and focused on Mary much more and much earlier than Western Christian communities did, but both share key themes relevant to the asexuality of Mary. One of those themes is establishing Mary's place in God's plans for Israel.

Early Christian texts are explicit about seeing Mary's miraculous conception of Jesus as the last, and greatest, of God's procreative interventions to protect and save his people. The Davidic lineage of Mary had been emphasized in works as early as the second century, establishing her as the descendant of the Hebrew Bible mothers. It is not surprising, then, that this theme was repeatedly elaborated in fourth-century Christian texts. Justin Martyr in second-century Palestine was one of the earliest to claim that Mary was of the tribe of Judah; he was not alone.[69] Yet interpretations that placed Mary within Israelite history did not stop there. Many other Hebrew Bible stories were interpreted to include Mary within them symbolically, or to establish the continuity of the mothers' and Mary's role in establishing their peoples' special status. In the fourth century, the bishop of Jerusalem, Cyril, became quite impatient with objections that were being expressed regarding Mary's virginal motherhood: "If they believe that God made fertile such sterile and aged wombs as that of Sarah, Abraham's wife, how could they hold that it was absurd for the same God to have made fertile, virginally, the young womb of Mary?"[70]

In fourth-century Syria, Gregory of Nyssa pointed to another Hebrew Bible image of Mary's virginal motherhood, when he compared Mary to the burning bush that Moses encountered in Exodus 3. (For those unfamiliar with the Exodus passage, this is a bush that burns but is not consumed, out of which God speaks to the prophet Moses). Gregory comments: "As on the mountain the bush burned but was not consumed, so the Virgin gave birth to the light and was not corrupted. Nor should you consider the comparison to the bush to be embarrassing, for it prefigures the God-bearing body of the Virgin.[71]"

Likewise, Severus of Antioch wrote of removing the sandals from his feet as he approached the Virgin Mother of God (as Moses had done when approaching the "holy ground" surrounding the burning bush within which God's presence resided).[72] John of Damascus in seventh-century Syria fused Jewish motifs from Genesis 18 with the Gospel birth narrative by explicitly equating Sarah's tent with Mary's womb:

> God, the Word, came to live in her [Mary's] womb as if beneath the tent of Abraham, human nature offered bread baked on the ashes, that is to say the first fruits of herself from her very pure blood, cooked and transformed into bread by the divine fire subsisting in her person, and truly serving as nourishment to a body made alive by a reasonable and intelligent soul.[73]

Thus, John used the Genesis 18 frame in order to convey a continuity between Jewish and Christian history, evident in the enduring and faithful intervention of God in the creation of his evolving people. Just as Sarah baked bread for God in her tent at Mamre and was promised and then given a son, so too Mary "baked bread"—the Bread of Life—in her "tent"/womb and also received a son from God. John forges this connection through explicit comparison, metaphor, and the theme of God's participation in the conception of his chosen sons.

Even more germane to our explorations, Ephrem the Syrian wrote a popular hymn in the fourth century that placed Mary directly in the line of Tamar and Ruth. However, in Ephrem's hymn Mary redefines and redeems the sexual transgressions of the earlier mothers. Note that Mary is speaking directly to Jesus in this passage.

> On your account [Jesus], women have hurried after men: Tamar desired a man who was widowed and Ruth loved a man who was old . . . Tamar went out and in darkness stole the light. And in impurity she stole holiness . . . *For it was a holy thing, the adultery of Tamar, for your sake* . . . She became a widow for your sake. It was you whom she coveted; *she ran and became—even a whore—for your sake* . . . Ruth, with a man on the threshing floor she lay down, for your sake. *Her love was bold for your sake* . . .[74]

This transformation of sexual transgressions into selfless devotion to a chosen son sounds like something a rabbi might have written, does it not? Like Lot's daughters, these bed-trickster mothers are understood in Ephrem's hymn to have been serving the long-term genealogical plans of God to send Jesus to humankind. Ephrem suggests that those plans are now made complete in Mary, as she creates a new Israel.

These are just a few examples of this widespread theme that links Mary to Jewish history and the Israelite mothers. Indeed, the cooptation of Jewish traditions abound in early Christianity. In the case of Mary, many Christian writers intentionally appropriated the Hebrew Bible God and his procreative interventions with Israel's mothers and used them to legitimate a new and "better" chosen son. The claim to a "better son" is not subtle in early Christian texts. To Athanasius in fourth-century Egypt, Mary is the new ark of the covenant[75] "containing *the true manna*,[76] that is, the flesh in which divinity resides."[77] For Gregory the Great in the seventh century, Mary's maternity is equal to God's parting of the Red Sea to save the Israelites through Moses. Mary—the new Moses—opens the way for a greater, once-for-all saving of God's people, through Jesus' death on the cross.

The point of these ubiquitous links back to Hebrew Bible stories is to establish that Mary—and her son—exceeded all prior mothers, miracles, and events.[78] Thus, Proclus of Constantinople in the fifth century could claim that Mary actually transformed the life stories of her Israelite foremothers, liberating them from the shame of Eve, erasing their own shame and rendering them free from censure:

> Eve has been healed; the Egyptian woman [Hagar] has been silenced . . . Sarah is acclaimed as the fertile field of peoples; Rebekah is honored as the able conciliator of blessings; Leah, too, is admired as mother of the ancestor [Judah] according to the flesh . . . Mary is venerated, because she became the Mother, the cloud, the bridal chamber, and *the ark of the Lord*.[79]

Let's pause here for a moment to take note of an important distinction that is made in this triumphalist passage. Proclus states that Mary is the ark of "the Lord," not the mother of an ancestor, like Judah, or any other righteous patriarch, but of the Lord God himself. Here is an extraordinary exceeding of Hebrew Bible motherhood. Reinforcing this radical claim, Mary was given the Greek title *Theotokos* ("Mother of God") by many church fathers. But how and why did the need for a divine child arise? Where did the story of Jesus' divinity come from?

There are many, many answers to this question. Some scholars point to popular understandings of divinity and humanity that were already around, in books and stories, when Christianity began. In this chapter, however, we are asking different questions. What *purpose* did the story of Jesus' divinity serve for the emerging Christian movement and what kind of radically new maternity was required to also serve that end? What kind of very different mother was required for this task? A new version of an Israelite mother was being used in Christian texts to define a new and better son. If the Hebrew Bible matriarchs were tasked with giving birth to chosen, Torah-observant, righteous sons who would lead their people in the ways of God, Mary was tasked with producing a very different son who would save a deeply sinful people.

To understand the early Christian need to establish the divinity of Mary's human child, we must make a short detour into some basic Jewish and Christian concepts. Reviewing these ideas will also be helpful to understanding how and why Mary's sexuality became even more central to the definition of Christian identity than the mothers' sexuality had been to Israelite identity. This will be especially helpful to those readers who are less familiar with Judaism and Christianity. While there was, and still is, a great deal of diversity *within* Judaism and Christianity, these are some fundamental ideas with which they began that remain central to this day.

Fundamentally, then, Israelite religion taught that following God's laws (Torah) was the best way to honor the people's covenant with God. This would keep them righteous in God's eyes and God near to them. This was linked to other ideals, such as the obligation to try to "repair" God's world through good deeds, which would also hasten the coming of the Jewish messiah. In the Jewish tradition, there was no need to be "saved" because the people were already chosen and loved by God; nonetheless, it was still their responsibility to honor and love God, and to be a blessing to the world. Otherwise, God's presence would withdraw from them.

In contrast, early Christianity—thanks to the influence of Augustine of Hippo—introduced the idea of "original sin," an intrinsic sinful nature which was passed down by Adam and Eve, the first human beings who sinned against God in the primeval garden of Eden.[80] Original sin, Augustine explained, was thence inevitably transmitted through every parent to their children, *through sexual reproduction.* (I will note here in passing that Jewish readings of Adam and Eve's expulsion from the garden do not discuss such an "original sin," but rather focus on the first couple's disobedience of God's commandments and the painful punishment that separation from God's presence entails.) Because of the doctrine of original sin, Christians were taught that they needed to be saved from their unavoidably sinful nature—which was transmitted through sexual intercourse—no matter who they were.

How to be saved, then? Early Christian doctrine taught that the only way to be saved was to believe in the gift of Jesus' death (sacrifice) on the cross, which paid for all human sins for all time. Christians inherited this idea from the Israelite practice of sacrificing animals to God at the Jerusalem temple to pay (atone) for any sins they had committed. For Christians, one had only to have faith that Jesus' sacrifice atoned for their sins. Of course, faith was only one step in a process that included the ritual of baptism—a symbolic self-sacrifice that stood for dying with Christ and rising as a new person—and *being born again* through the Holy Spirit (an important detail to which we will return in the next chapter).

For those not raised in the Christian faith, this may all seem a bit perplexing. However, for our purposes, there are two aspects of Mary's maternity and sexuality that are most necessary to maintaining these ideas: 1) The belief that sacrificial payment for sin only works if "like" is sacrificed for "like"; in this case, only *human* flesh can redeem, or pay for, *human* sins. Therefore, Jesus *had to be human*—had to have a human mother—in order to be a redeeming sacrifice that paid for humanity's sins. On the other hand, 2) the weight of human sin was too great for any human being to be able to bear so Jesus *had to be God* in order to have the strength and purity to bear God's wrath at the sinfulness of humanity.

In this way, we arrive at Mary's womb, which provides the necessary humanity of Jesus, while the divine nature of Jesus, the texts claim, is provided by God. By the fifth century, Christian orthodoxy had solidified this proposition into an official doctrinal "mystery": Jesus was 100 percent human and 100 percent divine, two natures in one person, inseparable yet unmixed. The Council of Chalcedon in 451 CE produced the orthodox Christian creed (or statement of belief) that pertains for many Christians to this day. It consolidated the work of several prior councils of bishops, and was crystal clear about Jesus' being, which, it said, should be,

> acknowledged as two natures, unconfused, unchanging, undivided, and without separation. The distinction of natures is in no way abolished on account of this union, but rather the characteristic property of each nature is preserved, and concurring into one Person and one subsistence, not as if Christ were parted or divided into two persons, but remains one and the same Son and Only-begotten God, Word, Lord, Jesus Christ.[81]

Now consider that Mary is the key to all these claims: she is the linchpin of human salvation, because she is the one who provides Jesus with his humanity.

Understanding how high the stakes were, and not forgetting the association of sin with sexual intercourse, it should now be very clear how and why the persistent question of female sexual organs, sexuality, and the moral disciplining of both became intensified in Mary's story. Jesus cannot be any human child; his mother cannot be any human mother. She must be worthy to hold divinity within her; she must be a worthy "ark." Scholarship on this question is extensive, to say the least. In this chapter we will look at just a few early Christian texts that focus on Mary's miraculous hymen, asking how they are similar and/or different from the Jewish commentaries on the Hebrew Bible mothers' hymens that we studied above. Like them, the discussions of Mary's hymen in this subset of Christian texts also reinforce the belief that mothers' reproductive acts separate people into chosen, saved, and disavowed "children."

CANNIBALIZING MARY'S FLESH

In early authoritative accounts of Jesus' conception an important claim was made that Jesus was created in two stages, or "two generations." What were these "generations"? One church father, Basil of Caesarea, described Jesus' first divine generation as follows. Quoting from the Gospel of John, he explained that Jesus was with the Father from the beginning of time, at the creation of the world:

> His origin was not from Mary, nor does he belong to her time. What, then? "In the beginning was the Word, and the Word

> was with God, and the Word was God." (John 1:1) [Jesus/the Word was] Eternal substance, impassable generation [forever unchanging], majesty of nature, which he possesses in union with the Father.[82]

This explanation should sound familiar to us. Such pre-Marian, heavenly conceptions of Jesus were also featured in the so-called marginal or "heretical" texts examined in chapter 3, Ode 19 and Oracle 8. Also like them, influential church fathers also described a second conception that took place in Mary. In the official orthodox version of this "second generation," Jesus' humanity—literally, his flesh—is "made" out of Mary's flesh, as Origen of Alexandria in the third century explains:

> In the case of any man, it is appropriate to say that he was born "by means of a woman," because before he was born of a woman, he took his origin from a man. But Christ, whose flesh did not take its origin from a man's seed, is rightly said to have been born "of a woman."[83]

To explain fully, Origen continues in the same text to cite a common understanding of conception and gestation in his culture. He argues that in normal cases women are just a receptacle, with the father providing *all* the matter of the child in a paternal sperm/embryo. However, in Jesus' case, his flesh had to come from his mother, since the paternal seed was spiritual. Hence, Mary's unique conception and gestation of Jesus entails her providing all the fleshly material for his body. Furthermore, and importantly, Origen notes that because Mary did not have sex to conceive, her flesh and Jesus' flesh are sinless. I wonder what would be left of Mary's body after it had been used to all these ends.

It was not just Origen who told this story. The same explanation of Jesus' human flesh is repeated many times, including by a later commentator, the fourth-century Epiphanius of Salamis, who puts it thus: "Jesus is both man and God at once . . . As man, he is truly born of Mary, having been begotten without manly seed . . . Without manly seed, *he made himself a holy body*, taking it from the *Theotokos* Mary."[84]

Thinking back again to the earlier, second-century Christian texts that we looked at in chapter 3, the question of agency (not to mention consent) may occur to you: *Who exactly* is creating Jesus' flesh? Is it Mary or is it Jesus? We have just seen that Origen in the third century described Mary as not just a receptacle, but the provider of Jesus' flesh. He notes that her sexual virginity is the cause of the sinlessness of Jesus' flesh. In contrast, Epiphanius in the fourth century described Jesus making a holy body for himself, preemptively taking the material for it from Mary. Meanwhile, Basil of Caesarea described Mary's body as "a workshop" that produced Jesus' humanity, yet Basil still identified "the active principles of this birth" as the Holy Spirit and the "overshadowing power of the Most High."[85] Mary does not "make" Jesus' flesh in Basil's account. Her own flesh is taken from her by Jesus and various other agents of God.

As time passes, and with few exceptions, the most important contribution that Mary makes to the generation of Jesus' sinless humanity is her asexuality, her utter lack of sexuality. It is her purity and her lack of physical congress with any man that secures the human savior that is required in the Christian economy of salvation. And this is where Mary's miraculous hymen enters the picture.

MARY'S HYMEN

The dominant position of the church fathers, across the early Christian centuries, was that Mary's hymen was never broken. The self-defloration that the Hebrew Bible mothers practiced in order to produce God's sons was apparently not necessary in Mary's case. The implication was, perhaps, that her sexual purity was not in question. Or was it? Even before the academic authoritative explanations that denied any hymen-breaking, there was a very early "gospel," *The Protoevangelium of James*, that provided a popular narrative. It included expressions of skepticism about Mary's virginity in childbirth and featured very memorable and dramatic proofs of Mary's virginity both before and after giving birth to Jesus. Was it "answering" popular skepticism about the Christian story of Mary's virginity? Certainly. This Gospel never made it into the official New Testament; indeed, by the fifth century, it had been rejected and condemned by the pope himself. Yet, many of its details were used to construct church doctrines still held today about Mary, her virginity, and miraculous childbearing.

We will here focus only on the part of the story that addressed the intact state of Mary's hymen during childbirth. This section begins with Mary in labor in a cave; she is experiencing no pain. Joseph goes for help while she is in labor and finds an Israelite midwife nearby. The midwife witnesses the childbirth from the entrance to the cave where "a bright cloud" overshadows it. When the cloud recedes, the baby Jesus is in Mary's arms. The midwife then declares that "salvation has come to Israel."[86] Leaving the cave, the midwife tells another woman named Salome what she has seen: "A virgin has given birth!"[87] Salome says she will not believe this until she has put her finger inside Mary and tested her condition. Back they go to the cave. Salome inserts her finger into Mary's vagina and her entire hand catches on fire: "And she cried out, saying, 'Woe for my lawlessness and the unbelief that made me test the living God. Look, my hand is falling away from me and being consumed in fire.'"[88] An angel appears and tells Salome to touch the baby Jesus; when she does, she is healed. Talk about discouraging questions or skepticism about Mary's hymen! This text depicts frightening consequences for anyone who doubts.

Of course, the church fathers went on to write complex commentaries on Mary's virginity. Only a few reach this level of drama. Some of them held that her hymen remained intact only during her conception of Jesus; some, that it remained so even during her birthing of Jesus; still others, that Mary remained a virgin "perpetually," even after Jesus was born.

In the case of Mary's hymen at conception, alternative explanations became popular, for instance that the conception was accomplished verbally, and not physically. Thus, in a fourth-century sermon on the annunciation the angel Gabriel speaks directly to Mary, saying,

> *And behold, you will conceive in your womb.* The accomplishment of this preceded my [Gabriel's] word; the mysterious conception was faster than my voice. You already carry within you, in your womb, the Lord, the Creator of all things who, from your holy and uncontaminated flesh, is building the temple of his holy flesh without any difficulty.[89]

The angel explains that his words impregnated Mary, thus leaving her flesh, including her hymen, "holy and uncontaminated." Athanasius, a great champion of virginity in Christian women, is one among many who extended this erasure of bodily penetration to Mary's *birthing* of Jesus, arguing "Neither did she lose her virginity when she gave the Savior to the world; to the contrary, she preserved it intact, like a precious treasure."[90] Caelius Sedulis, an Italian priest and hymnist of the fifth century, goes further, suggesting that the baby Jesus protected her hymen as he moved through the birth canal, essentially making Mary's virginity her son's doing: "Then the most-high Infant, conserving intact the womb of his temple, left undamaged the pathways of his birth. He who was born bears witness for the Virgin: He left her closed coming in and closed in coming forth."[91]

Nonetheless, this concerted testimony to Mary's intact hymen and virginity, while it was dominant and became increasingly so over time, was not unanimous. Indeed, there were disagreements amongst early Christians (and not just writers or church leaders) about whether Jesus was born, or had a human body, at all. As you now know, such questions presented a real threat to the ability of Jesus to save humanity through his *human* sacrifice on the cross. Therefore, in the face of these speculations, two very influential scholars of the Western Christian tradition—Tertullian and Jerome—switched strategies, claiming that Mary's hymen *was* broken during childbirth by a very human, very physical baby Jesus. Jerome wrote more than a hundred years after Tertullian, but his version of this claim is simpler, so we will start with him.

Jerome was a priest, theologian, and historian, and one of the greatest Western Christian scholars of the fourth and fifth centuries. He held an orthodox view regarding Mary's virginity both during the conception and after Jesus was born. His claim was based on his trust that the Scriptures said it was so. The Bible said that Mary was a virgin when she conceived and did *not* say she had conjugal sex with Joseph after Jesus was born: "We do not deny what is written . . . we *do* reject what is *not* written."[92]

On the other hand, however, Jerome was utterly dismissive of the possibility that Mary remained a virgin when she delivered Jesus. In fact, he offered a graphic description of the physical "humiliations" that Mary and Jesus underwent during childbirth. He tongue-lashed opponents who "blushed" at the idea that "God was born by passing through the genital organs of a Virgin."[93] He forced the reality of birthing and postpartum bodies upon his opponents: "the nausea, the birth, the blood, the swaddling clothes."[94]

Why would Jerome, who was so interested in establishing Mary's perpetual virginity (even after Jesus was born), take this detour into the fleshly reality of childbirth? It appears in the text that he did this to explicitly drive home Jesus' humanity, precisely his fitness to be a sacrifice for human sin (human flesh for human sin) mentioned above: "We do not blush; we are not silent about these matters. The greater the humiliations he suffered for me, *the greater my debt to him*."[95] A greater debt existed because Jesus' humanity was created expressly for the purpose of being sacrificed and redeeming human sinners. In the end, Jerome even reasserted Mary's virginity postpartum, broken hymen and all. How? He argued that her abstention from sex, and not the state of her hymen, was what defined her virginity.[96] Sexuality was more than a physical state in Jerome's argument; it was a moral barometer that established the purity of her body and spirit.

If we think back to judgements on the Hebrew Bible matriarchs and their self-deflorations, we will recall a similar logic at work. In rabbinic texts, the matriarchs broke their own hymens, but only for a greater good. Their desire and intentions were towards mothering chosen sons and not sexuality, regardless of the state of their hymens. In addition, the very need to deflower themselves demonstrated their prior virginity, acting as testimony to the purity of their bodies and minds. Their sexuality was thus safely contained. They were not ordinary women; they did not engage in immoral sexual activity before motherhood; their birthing was not common; their children were chosen.

Even before Jerome adopted this logic, however, it appeared in an earlier, even more graphic examination of Mary's body and childbirth, in one of the earliest writers of Latin Christianity, Tertullian. As indicated above, Tertullian wrote a good century *before* Jerome. In fact, Jerome wrote a biography of this third-century predecessor, Tertullian, at the end of the fourth century. It is quite probable, then, that Jerome had read Tertullian's discussion of Mary's hymen and that it influenced his later writing about Mary's broken hymen. Thus, we are turning to the "parent" text that may have given birth to Jerome's interpretations.

Tertullian was situated in North Africa and was a prominent denouncer of Christian "heresies"—that is, he vilified and prohibited Christian beliefs that fell outside an emerging set of correct beliefs (orthodoxy). Yet, Christianity was still extraordinarily diverse in the third century and so this "orthodoxy" was quite unstable and often contested. Thus, the battle to impose it on all Christians was extremely severe, often brutal in tone.

Ironically, while enforcing this supposed orthodox consensus and condemning "bad" Christians, Tertullian proceeded to undermine that very consensus by disagreeing with other church fathers about Mary's hymen. I suggested above that this had become necessary because "heretics" were claiming that Jesus had no physical body. Thus, we find Tertullian insisting that Mary's hymen was broken during childbirth. In two separate anti-heretical works, *Against Marcion* and *On the Flesh of Christ,* both written during the early decades of the third century, Tertullian graphically discussed Mary's hymen, indeed, all her reproductive organs. The arguments he made were critical to the question of Mary's sexuality because they include extremely raw, visceral depictions of the maternal body and childbearing, depictions that reveal deep disgust with the female body, sexual reproduction, and childbirth.[97] To be sure, this attitude was part of Tertullian's culture. Yet, Tertullian had a problem. He had to defend Jesus' *human birth*—including its physical impact on Mary's hymen—precisely *because* he was responding to Christians who believed that Jesus was a spiritual being only. For them, Jesus only *appeared* to have a human body.

Such a "bad" Christian was Marcion, whose arguments were widely read in and beyond his region of Pontus (present-day northeastern Turkey). For Marcion, Jesus was *not* the Jewish messiah, but rather a spiritual entity sent by a new God (a better God than the God of the Hebrew Bible) to teach human beings how to escape the evil material world. *Against Marcion* was Tertullian's multivolume denunciation of these beliefs. In this work, we see Tertullian navigating prevailing negative attitudes towards sexuality and the female body—attitudes into which he himself was surely socialized—in order to satisfy the Christian need for a pure, yet fleshly Jesus, who could redeem humanity. How did he go about this?

One of Tertullian's strategies was to attribute extremely negative views of the female womb, pregnancy, and childbirth *to his opponent*, Marcion, and then, ultimately, to denounce such attitudes as completely misunderstanding the doctrine of Jesus as a *human* redeemer of humanity. In this excerpt, Tertullian reveals that Marcion sees the female womb as a sewer:

> Come then, wind up your cavils [objections] against *the most sacred and reverend works of nature*; inveigh against all that you are; destroy the origin of flesh and life; *call the womb a sewer* of the illustrious animal—in other words, the manufactory for the production of man; dilate on the impure and shameful tortures of parturition [childbirth], and then on the *filthy, troublesome, contemptible issues of the puerperal [birth] labor* itself![98]

Notice the contrasting views of gestation and childbirth in this passage as both "the most sacred and reverend works of nature" and filthy, contemptible sewage. This double message—childbirth is sacred and it's filthy—sums up well Tertullian's dilemma, *and* the uneven way that he tried to solve it. For all the time that he was rhetorically condemning Marcion's disgust with wombs and childbirth, he was simultaneously recreating the same horrified vision of them in his own text. Ironically, his text brings to life the disgust that he condemned.[99]

Another of Tertullian's strategies was to use Jesus' words in the Gospels to condemn Marcion's anti-body and anti-birth argument. In the quotation Tertullian used (Mark 8:38/Luke 9:26), Jesus is talking to his disciples and says, "For whoever is ashamed of me and of my words in this adulterous and sinful generation, of him will the Son of man also be ashamed, when he comes in the glory of his Father with the holy angels." In the Gospels, Jesus has just predicted his death on the cross—understood as a shameful way to die in first-century Judea. Tertullian applies Jesus' words to his human *birth*, which would also make others feel ashamed of him. No God should or could become human and remain a god. It was beneath a god. Tertullian then turns these words on Marcion. He points out that, according to Marcion, Jesus was never born at all, so no one would have a reason to feel shame in Marcion's Jesus. Therefore, Marcion's version of Jesus is not the Gospels' Jesus:

> But how can that Christ of yours be liable to a shame, which it is impossible for him to experience? Since he was never condensed

> into human flesh in the womb of a woman, although a virgin; never grew from human seed, although only after the law of corporeal substance, from the fluids of a woman; was never deemed flesh before shaped in the womb; never called fetus after such shaping; was never delivered from a ten months' writhing in the womb; was never shed forth upon the ground, amidst the sudden pains of parturition, *with the unclean issue which flows at such a time through the sewerage of the body*, forthwith to inaugurate the light of life with tears, and with that primal wound which severs the child from her who bears him; never received the copious ablution, nor the meditation of salt and honey; nor did he initiate a shroud with swaddling clothes; *nor afterwards did he ever wallow in his own uncleanness, in his mother's lap*; nibbling at her breast.[100]

By this point, Tertullian was not even denying the shame and disgust that women's flesh, wombs, and bodily fluids evoked; indeed, he reinforced them. In an incisive essay on Tertullian, biblical scholar Jennifer Glancy refers to this reinforcing effect as Tertullian's "mire-wallowing." She notes, "Vocabularies of moral deficiency and human waste overlap with the vocabulary of gestation and birth. Tertullian describes the pre-natal environment as a latrine."[101] It is certainly hard to ignore how Tertullian describes Jesus being spewed out on the ground in a liquid mess of afterbirth and blood, and then wallowing in his own feces on Mary's lap. In Tertullian's texts, Glancy notes, "Wombs are dirty places, and womb-bearers are dirty people . . . Tertullian wallows in the filthiness of flesh."[102]

This was a strategy that he was to repeat in his treatise entitled *On the Flesh of Christ*, written at about the same time. It includes another denunciation of Marcionite claims. In *On the Flesh*, Tertullian again pointed out how wrong it was to despise Jesus' and Mary's flesh/bodies, even as he reproduced the language of disgust. Speaking directly to Marcion, Tertullian writes:

> Come now, beginning from the nativity itself, declaim against the *uncleanness* of the generative elements within the womb, *the filthy concretion of fluid and blood*, of the growth of the flesh for nine months long out of *that very mire . . . This reverend course of nature*, you, O Marcion, spit upon; and yet, in what way were you born? You detest a human being at his birth; then after what fashion do you love anybody?[103]

Notice how, again in this passage, Tertullian refers to gestation and childbirth as a "reverend course of nature," implying that he held a positive view of human reproduction. However, this view only exists at an abstract level. It is forcefully contradicted by his descriptions of the actual mechanics of reproduction. He offers no such language of sacredness or reverence regarding the female body, the womb, or amniotic fluids. As Glancy succinctly observes: "Despite Tertullian's initial evocation of parturition as a sacred and reverend work of nature, he insists on exposing explicitly excremental and shameful associations of pregnancy and childbirth for both mother and child."[104]

Tertullian's endgame with all of this is quite clear, as I've suggested above. He had to argue that Jesus was completely immersed in the "filth" of human fleshliness—this had to be graphically made clear—in order to argue that Jesus redeemed filthy human flesh. The sacrifice of "like" for "like" accomplished through Jesus' crucifixion was behind it all. Jesus was not exclusively spiritual as a being. He was unequivocally flesh and blood. It was only Mary's virginity that made his flesh and blood pure and sinless.

There remains one more, very popular Marian theme to discuss, one that directly bears on our exploration of the mothers' sexuality. This theme also emerged out of Tertullian's graphic depictions of Jesus in his mother's body and is one I find especially difficult to read. One of the most consequential images of Mary that has persisted over time is the idea of Mary as the spouse—the wife—of Christ. It initially emerged out of Tertullian's text below in which Jesus breaks his mother's hymen as he exits her womb. You read that right. Jesus deflowers his mother. Please note that the Latin word, *uulua*, that Tertullian used in this passage is translated below as "womb," however, it also carries the meaning of vagina, so what is being broken is almost certainly in the vagina, not the womb. It is worth citing in full.

> She who bare (really) bare; and *although she was a virgin when she conceived, she was a wife when she brought forth her son.* Now, as a wife, she was under the very law of "opening the womb," wherein it was quite immaterial whether the birth of the male was by virtue of a husband's co-operation or not; it was the same sex [male] that opened her womb. Indeed, hers is the womb on account of which it is written of others also: "Every male that opens the womb shall be called holy to the Lord." For who is really holy but the Son of God? Who properly opened the womb but He who opened a closed one? But it is marriage which opens the womb in all cases. The virgin's womb, therefore, was especially opened because it was especially closed. Indeed, she ought rather to be called "not a virgin" than "a virgin," becoming a mother at a leap, as it were, before she was a wife. And what must be said more on this point? Since it was in this sense that the apostle declared that the Son of God was born not of

> a virgin, but "of a woman," he in that statement recognized the condition of the "opened womb" which ensues in marriage.[105]

In this passage, Tertullian defined the breaking of Mary's hymen in legal terms: "the law of opening the womb." In doing this, he explicitly tied together marriage, male penetration as the means of opening wombs, being a wife, and being a mother.

In this passage, Tertullian sanctified the sexuality implied by intercourse within marriage by saying that God had declared the opening of the womb holy: "Every male that opens the womb shall be called holy to the Lord." Interestingly, in Tertullian's argument, this biblical quotation appears to include husbands' penetration ("It is marriage that opens the womb in all cases"). However, the actual Scriptural verses which Tertullian was citing—Exodus 13:2 and Luke 2:22–23—are focused entirely on the firstborn son that "opens the womb." In Exodus 13, God is instructing Moses about what the Israelites should sacrifice or dedicate to him. He commands, "Consecrate to me all the firstborn. Whatever is the first to open the womb among the Israelites, of human beings and animals, is mine." Note that it is the *firstborn,* and not the *first penetrator* that God deems holy. Luke, centuries later, cites this same Exodus verse in his Gospel, applying it to Jesus as a sacrifice, the one who will be dedicated to God, and prefiguring Jesus' sacrifice on the cross. The quotation appears just as the adolescent Jesus arrives at the temple to be presented to God: "When the time came for their purification according to the law of Moses, they brought him up to Jerusalem to present him to the Lord (as it is written in the law of the Lord, 'Every firstborn male shall be designated as holy to the Lord')."

Again, it is the *firstborn* that is dedicated to the Lord. Furthermore, in Luke, no mention of a hymen or womb is in sight. The body of Jesus' mother is not at issue in this Gospel passage. Nonetheless, by weaving together God's commands in the Bible with the ideas of marriage, birth, and sacrifice to God, Tertullian created a rich and enlarged intersection of meanings, beyond the original purposes of the verses. Bringing them together, Tertullian artfully fused the palpably physical humanity of a Jesus that breaks his mother's hymen with the painfully physical humanity of his death on the cross. Through that same flesh, in both cases, he is the holy sacrifice that God demands. This is intellectually sophisticated, I concede.

And yet I cannot, nor do I wish to, lose sight of the fact that in Tertullian's hands Mary's body has been penetrated and her hymen broken (inside out or not) by her own son. This is not just an esoteric scholarly argument about *what* Jesus was. It is also a description of the deflowering of a mother by her son. Even though Tertullian's description of Jesus breaking Mary's hymen was not dominant in the early church, it was not without influence. His contemporary, Origen of Alexandria, who was also well-respected and influential, took up the same argument in his commentary on Luke 2:23. It's possible, though less clear, that he also thought Jesus broke his mother's hymen during childbirth, though he did soften these images by insisting on the holiness of Mary's body:

> In the case of every other woman, it is not the birth of an infant but intercourse with a man that opens the hymen/womb. But the hymen/womb of the Lord's mother was opened at the time when her offspring was brought forth, because before the birth of Christ a male did not even touch her hymen/womb, holy as it was and deserving of all respect.[106]

The identification of Mary as the wife of her son is *not* present in Origen's text; it was hinted at in Tertullian's account. Origen renders Mary's deflowering in the passive tense, "was opened," without identifying who opened. It is Tertullian who explicitly linked Mary's broken hymen to a kind of reverse intercourse with her son. In his text, sexuality and celibacy, virginity and womanhood are conflated. The effect is that sexuality and womanhood are erased, modified, and reformed, recreated as celibacy and virginity in Mary's body.

Thus, early church leaders grappled with, and spiritualized, the theme of Mary as wife of Christ. Yet, their authoritative, official "spin" on Mary's sexuality, her hymen, and the relationship of God and Jesus to her body were simply not controllable. There were many Jewish parodies, as well as Christian texts, that featured sexual humor and innuendo around Mary's conception and Jesus' birth. Nowhere is this tendency more vibrant than in the fifteenth-century English N-Town Plays, a series of forty-two popular plays based loosely on the Bible that were performed, from town to town, by traveling actors. Often the plays were performed in synch with holy days in the church's calendar. For instance, the fifteenth play, "Procession to Calvary & Crucifixion of Christ," would be performed around the church's observance of Good Friday, the day Jesus was killed by the Romans, or the thirty-sixth play, "Christ's Appearance to the Three Marys," around Easter, the celebration of Jesus rising from the dead.

Mary plays a pronounced role in the N-Town cycle of plays, both in elevated respectful ways and in bawdy popular ways. The latter no doubt was intended to relieve doubts and anxieties about Mary's unusual pregnancy, including some passages filled with double meanings that are sexual and earthy. One particular scene in the play "The Annunciation" is forever merged in my mind with Tertullian's insistence on Jesus' reverse defloration of his mother, as it describes the annunciation scene as one of bawdy sexual consummation. Medieval scholar Emma Maggie Solberg encapsulates the dynamic well:

> The Holy Ghost arranges the match between Jesus and Mary, telling Jesus, "I, Love, to your lover shall lead you." Jesus takes on the role of the eager bridegroom, chastising . . . Gabriel for taking too long to allow him access to Mary's body, for which he yearns: "I have so great haste to be man there/In that meekest and purest virgin."[107]

Jesus cannot wait to get inside Mary. The double entendre is obvious and meant to be hilarious. As if this were not enough, as things progress the Holy Ghost asks Gabriel to give two tokens to Mary. One is the knowledge that her cousin Elizabeth will also miraculously become pregnant. *The other is orgasmic pleasure*. The Holy Ghost explains, "Her body shall be so fulfilled with bliss/That she shall soon think this sound incredible." Finally, Mary herself, when she is penetrated with rays of celestial light by the Father, Son, and Holy Ghost, cries out, "I cannot tell what joy, what bliss/Now I feel in my body!"[108] Of course, the double meanings go in both directions. While the scene may play on the sexuality of intercourse and conception, the higher meaning, the higher spiritual bliss is also understood and celebrated. Mary's experience is as spiritual as it is carnal. The audience's laughter and joy are both as well.

Meanwhile, within church teachings, the wife-of-Christ motif that Tertullian created would endure and proliferate in Christian tradition, becoming one of the most popular ways of talking about the relationship not just between Mary and Jesus, but also between an idealized Christian church and the resurrected Christ. We will discuss this in the next chapter. Even amongst the church fathers, however, it was a complicated concept with worrisome implications. For instance, just a few centuries after Tertullian wrote, Peter Chrysologus, an Italian archbishop, apparently felt that he had to reconcile Mary's simultaneous status as the wife of her husband, Joseph, *and* her son, Jesus. The tone of Peter's discussion is apologetic ("he [Jesus] did not steal anyone else's [wife]"). Referring to Mary as "God's spouse," he wrote:

> The messenger [angel] flies swiftly to the spouse [Mary], in order *to remove every attachment to a human marriage from God's spouse*. He does not take the Virgin away from Joseph but simply restores her to Christ, *to whom she had been promised when she was being formed in her mother's womb*. Christ, then, takes his own bride; he does not steal anyone else's. Nor does he cause

> any separation when he unites *his own creature* to himself, in a single body.[109]

Any human attachment to Joseph, including the sexuality that is implied in the word "marriage," had to be severed and a justification provided for doing so. If any semblance of Mary's consent to being impregnated ever existed in earlier texts, it is certainly gone here. Jesus' "taking" of Mary is justified because she is his "creature," "promised" to him in her own mother's womb, before even breathing her first breath. She is "united" to him "in a single body." Mary exists, then, *as* Jesus' body, even before her own body is formed in her mother's womb. The spiritualization and mystification of this "miracle" obscures—indeed prohibits or makes sacrilegious—speaking the truth of what happens to Mary. Within the Christian faith, the intention is that she be understood only in service to a narrative that existed long before she was in her mother's womb. I, however, will speak what I see. Mary's flesh is not her own. Whether it is a matter of stripping her of her natural sensuality and bodily pleasure or erasing her body completely as it becomes Jesus' body, she has been cannibalized.

DON'T ASK, DON'T TELL

Perhaps it was passages like these, and the mystifying concepts they struggled to express that led many church fathers to adopt a "don't ask, don't tell" policy in their writings on the conception and birth of Jesus. On the subject of Mary's conception of Jesus and Jesus' birth, the church fathers began to press their congregations and readers towards faith, and away from questioning. Thus, Chrysostom in the fourth century preached, "Do not pry into the mystery, but humbly accept what God has revealed, and do not be curious about what God keeps hidden,"[110] and, "Do not look for conformity with the natural order of things, since what has happened transcends the natural order . . ."[111] and "We remain silent about the how of both; we are not capable of expressing it."[112] He was certainly not alone. In yet another fourth-century sermon on the annunciation, Mary asks no fewer than six urgent questions to the angel in quick succession, including whether the laws of procreation will change for everyone, or just for her. Have the very laws of procreation been modified? To which the angel replies:

> You have understood who the Artisan is, do not be curious as to how; you have understood who the Sculptor is, do not ask questions about the work. You have heard that the holy spirit is involved; leave the fulfillment of the work to the spirit.[113]

Absolutely. Do not, any of you, inquire too deeply into what happened to Mary.

This insistence that Mary's conception and Jesus' birth are inexpressible and beyond human reason proliferates in many Christian texts. One of the most interesting to me comes at the end of the fifth to early sixth centuries in an anonymous Greek hymn. The hymnist sings to Mary directly and the refrain to each verse is "Hail! Bride Unbrided." In this hymn, we see that the wife-of-Christ theme was surfacing in hymns and worship services and not just in the scholarly treatises of educated church fathers. In the passage I am interested in, the hymnist tells Mary that the most eloquent become as dumb as fishes before her, then continues to greet her repeatedly, saying:

> Hail! confounder of the wise.
> Hail! making babble of men's eloquence.
> Hail! for the deep thinkers are made foolish.
> Hail! for the makers of myth have failed.
> Hail! thou who rends the word-webs of Athens . . .[114]

Clearly, philosophers ("word-web weavers of Athens") were writing critiques of the church fathers' arguments about Mary and Jesus. Indeed, the mystery of a deity being incarnated (made flesh) was ridiculed by Greco-Roman writers through the early centuries of the church. In such historical cultural hostilities, I see the early roots of the still active confrontation between logic, philosophy, science, and faith that we know today. In this hymn, I see a response that is still used today by Christians who are confronted with scientific arguments, for instance about Jesus' miracles: "These are mysteries. You can only understand Jesus' being through faith. Even then, human beings cannot fully understand." What is particularly interesting here is that, in this sixth-century hymn, it is Mary's body that purportedly stands against the words of the great philosophers of the age, yet it is not her maternal body at all, but rather God's actions on her body that defeat the philosophers.

I wish to make just one final observation to bring this chapter to a close. It relates to the regulation of belief that is apparent in the "don't ask, don't tell" arguments of the church fathers that we've just looked at. What began in the early centuries as an intellectual exploration amongst highly educated church fathers about what Jesus *was*, quickly became an insistence on a doctrine that had to be believed by all Christians—a truth that had to be acknowledged "through faith," whether they understood it or not. Thus, Ambrose of Milan in the fourth century would write: "If one does not believe that he [Jesus] has come, neither will he believe that he has taken flesh . . . Whoever denies this truth is a Manichee [heretic], a denier of Christ's flesh; for this reason he will not receive the remission of sins."[115] Anyone who did not believe in Jesus' humanity through Mary would be denied salvation through the church.

Ambrose was not an exception. During the fourth and fifth centuries, the church fathers were consolidating belief and institutionalizing it across Western and Eastern Christianity. Thus, Gregory Nazianzen in the East wrote an even more forceful warning to independently thinking Christians:

> If anyone does not admit that holy Mary is Mother of God (*Theotokos*), he is *cut off from the Godhead.* If anyone claims that Christ merely passed through Mary, as if passing through a channel, but denies that he was formed within her in a divine way (because there was no intervention of a man), and in a human way (that is, according to the laws of conception), he is *equally godless* . . . If anyone introduces the notion of two sons, one born of God the Father and the other born of the Mother, instead of a single and identical Son, *let him be deprived of the adoption of sons* [by God], promised to those who believe aright.[116]

Note that Gregory wrote this in a letter to a priest, Cledonicus, someone on the "front lines" so to speak, who was presumably then enforcing Gregory's version of orthodoxy amongst his church members. Marian scholar Luigi Gambero recently has written from a Catholic perspective, approving of Gregory's tactics and message, and summing up the letter as follows:

> Our author *rightly* holds . . . that the dogma of Mary's divine motherhood is the linchpin of the Church's doctrine about the incarnate Word and the mystery of human salvation. The text mentions nearly all of the most dangerous *errors* about the Incarnation; Mary appears as a point of reference that helps *us* eliminate heretical threats to the truth.

I greatly respect Gambero's research on how Mary was portrayed by the church fathers in the early centuries of the church. Indeed, I have relied on him throughout much of this chapter. Yet, I think it's important to point out that Gambero's present-day approval of Gregory's enforcement of "the Church's doctrine" against "dangerous errors" demonstrates the continuing success of the early church fathers in establishing a set of beliefs still attested by Christians today.

This is not to even mention the several fourth- and fifth-century councils of bishops that composed official statements of beliefs that all Christians were to adhere to and repeat in worship services. These councils were also historical "culture wars" that aimed to establish consensus by condemning those who "lost" the argument. When the dust settled, the councils produced "creeds" from the Latin, *credo*, which means "I believe." Statements cursing those who denied the truth of the Nicene and Constantinopolitan creeds were added to them when they were disseminated to Christians. Thus did Mary become the Mother of God over the course of the first centuries of the church. Thus were her body, her asexuality, and her abject obedience used to consolidate and impose a set of beliefs about sin and salvation that would establish the superiority of her son, *and* definitively and finally separate Christians from their Jewish brothers and sisters.

What a long road Mary has been led along, so far away now from the humanity and moxie of her Jewish foremothers. They could not speak for her, nor can I. She is just not available to us; she is not visible beyond the ways she has been used. Nevertheless, the words of Donna Kate Rushin's famous 1981 poem resound in my mind, and I will add them here, to weave my own thread into the web of meanings ascribed to Mary. AND MARY SAID:

> I've had enough
> I'm sick of seeing and touching both sides of things
> Sick of being the damn bridge for everybody . . .
> I'm sick of filling in your gaps
> Sick of being your insurance against
> The isolation of your self-imposed limitations
> Sick of being the crazy at your holiday dinners
> Sick of being the odd one at your Sunday Brunches
> Sick of being the sole Black friend to 34 individual White people
> Find another connection to the rest of the world
> Find something else to make you legitimate
> Find some other way to be political and hip
> I will not be the bridge to your womanhood, your manhood, your humanness
> I'm sick of reminding you not to close off too tight for too long
> I'm sick of mediating with your worst self on behalf on your better selves
> I am sick of having to remind you to breathe
> Before you suffocate your own fool self
> Forget it, stretch or drown, evolve or die
> The bridge I must be is the bridge to my own power
> I must translate my own fears
> Mediate my own weakness
> I must be the bridge to nowhere but my true self
> And then I will be useful.[117]

6

Holy Mother Church: From the Womb to the Baptismal Font

Howsoever I may view Mary and her fate, the early church had its own ideas. The church fathers determined that the apex of God's genealogical plans for his chosen people was to be found in the body of Mary and in the person of her transhuman son, Jesus. Mary was the ultimate Israelite matriarch, "a virgin not only in body, but in her mind,"[118] whose pregnancy was more miraculous than any before in the history of Israel. Jesus was the god-man, who saved sinners through his human flesh and divine power, thus far surpassing any prior Abrahamic or Davidic patriarch. It seems that the task was accomplished, the Israelite mothers and their chosen sons had been replaced "once for all."

Yet, if our explorations have taught us nothing else, they have demonstrated that the story is never over when it comes to God, mothers, and chosen or elect peoples. So, we turn now and ask: "what happens to the mother of God, postpartum?" There is so little in the New Testament to flesh out her motherhood, much less her personhood. What could possibly have been useful once the church fathers had dissected her reproductive body like a moth pinned to corkboard? She had served her purpose, birthing a god made flesh; she had been taken up to heaven. What was left to say? Did she survive in people's minds? Did she matter? Of course, the answer to these questions is yes.

Even the most cursory of investigations reveal, for instance, that Mary regularly appears in popular culture contexts. Most people, whether they are Christian or not, are aware of at least some mainstream images of Mary. Scary movies, for instance, may feature a character in dire circumstances mumbling the "Hail Mary" prayer. News stories feature Virgin Mary apparitions around the world. Indeed, one such story is the subject of a recent Amazon Prime Video film entitled "Fatima," which dramatizes the real-life story of three young shepherds' 1917 visions of the Virgin Mary in Portugal. Or again, around Christmas many people may attend worship services in churches or concerts in secular settings that include musical arrangements of the *Ave Maria* (Hail Mary) or the *Magnificat*.

Meanwhile, within Christian communities, the Hail Mary prayer is a staple of Roman Catholic Christian spirituality: "Hail Mary, Full of Grace, The Lord is with thee. Blessed art thou among women, and blessed is the fruit of thy womb, Jesus. Holy Mary, Mother of God, pray for us sinners now, and at the hour of death." In the Catholic, Eastern Orthodox, and Coptic Orthodox Christian churches, many annual feast days are celebrated in Mary's honor. These commemorate important moments in Mary's life, such as her birth, the annunciation, the conception of Jesus, her sorrow at the cross, and the assumption of her body into heaven.

Beyond Christian contexts, many travelers will have toured European cathedrals dedicated to Mary and learned that devotion to her greatly intensified during the Middle Ages. Probably the most well-known of such cathedrals is Notre Dame ("Our Lady") Cathedral in Paris, which recently burned.

All this visibility, devotion, and infatuation is not accidental, nor is the continuing importance of Mary in the spiritual lives of Christians of all stripes. A number of scholars over the years have pointed to the basic psychological need in human beings for a mother, for maternal power and protection, as one explanation for the rise of Marian devotion at certain points in church history. This may be true, as far as it goes, yet it fails to explain why Mary never became more primary or central. She did not become equal to, much less more powerful than, her father-God and savior-son. No. Such possibilities were carefully managed. The potential for such unrestricted elevation of Mary seems to have prompted some church fathers to be very explicit about Mary's subordinate position in Christian life and Christian salvation. Such early church moves to control the image of, and devotion to, Mary are important to us because we are not exploring people's psychological needs in this book, but rather how Christian culture has exploited such needs. Our method is mapping, absorbing, and responding to ongoing interpretations of biblical mothers—in this case, Mary.

With that in mind, I would like to begin by repeating that Mary's continued importance was and is not an accident. Mary did not fade into the background like, say, Tamar. Why? Clearly, the church fathers continued to find her virginity, motherhood, and central role in the salvation of humankind useful. As they separated Jesus followers from their Jewish and Pagan roots, they constructed a set of "correct" beliefs and behaviors for their followers. In this chapter, we will look at texts that elevated, denied, or co-opted Mary's power and status. In the case of co-optation, the church fathers transferred Mary's maternal power to the church itself, claiming for the church alone her central role in salvation. No human mother was required any longer. I must, however, offer a caveat here. While it may appear that such interpretive strategies represent a linear progression from elevation to negation to cooptation of Mary's power, this is not the case. As has been true with all the mothers' stories, the "conversation" between interpreters of Mary has gone back and forth, and continues to do so, returning to earlier claims or challenging them according to the ever-changing challenges that the church faces.

MARY: MOTHER, MEDIATOR, AND CO-REDEEMER

Let us begin by speaking of such a historical challenge and the need it created for elevated claims about Mary. In the face of much scoffing and skepticism about a "virgin conception," the church fathers intensified their idealization of Mary, her asexuality, and her physical virginity. Greek philosophers and Jewish writers alike ridiculed the claim that Mary was a virgin. In the second-century *Dialogue with Trypho,* Justin Martyr (a philosopher who converted to Christianity) and Trypho (a traditional Jew) argue about the virgin birth. Trypho calls the idea foolishness and tells Justin he has been overly influenced by Greek myths that feature gods impregnating virgins:

> In the fables of those who are called Greeks, it is written that Perseus was begotten of Danae, who was a virgin; he who is called among them Zeus having descended on her in the form of a golden shower. And you ought to feel ashamed when you make assertions similar to theirs, and rather say that Jesus was born man of men.[119]

Another example can be found in a fictional account created by the second-century philosopher Celsus, in which Celsus imagined a dialogue between Jesus and a Jewish opponent. In this cutting exchange, Jesus' opponent accuses him of having made up the story of his virgin birth. According to the opponent, Mary became pregnant through adultery with a Roman soldier named Panthera and she was rejected by Joseph. Jesus was thus an illegitimate child whose poverty forced him into servitude in Egypt, where he learned magic. He then returned to Palestine performing "miracles"

(Egyptian magic) and claiming he was a god. Jesus' opponent sarcastically notes, "Odd that the kingdom of God, the core of [Christian] teaching, is made to hang on the disgrace [extramarital pregnancy] of a rejected woman, whose husband turned her aside."[120]

Such counter-narratives to the Gospel stories that focused on how Mary got pregnant flourished over the years, perhaps most memorably in the parody *Toledot Yeshu* (*The Life of Jesus*), of which there were many versions. The tale appeared first in oral stories starting around the fourth century and then in written texts from about the ninth century on. These stories included details such as Jesus being the product of rape and adultery and Mary actively menstruating during his conception. Yet another example is found in a Jewish anti-Christian text entitled *Nizzahon Vetus*. This fourteenth-century critique is focused on Mary, Jesus, and childbirth. You may note that it sounds quite like Tertullian in its content, even though it lacks the ultimate turn to Tertullian's professed approval of the flesh. In place of approval, it includes a rabbinic explanation for the *impurity* of amniotic and menstrual fluids based in Torah:

> How can this man be God, for he entered a woman with a stomach full of feces who frequently sat him down in the privy during the nine months, and when he was born he came out dirty and filthy, wrapped in a placenta and defiled by the blood of childbirth and impure issue. The Torah, on the other hand, warns against approaching a menstruate woman, a woman who has had an impure issue, and one who has just given birth, as it is written, ". . . she shall touch no hallowed thing . . . until the day of her purification be fulfilled" (Lev. 12:4). Hence, he was not worthy of association with anything sacred.[121]

The many denunciations by church fathers of such attacks on the virgin birth and the maternal body, and the many impassioned pronouncements about Mary's pristine body that we saw in chapter 5, certainly make sense in light of these parodies. The fathers' outraged defenses were not, however, the only method of countering Pagan and Jewish humor about Mary. From early on and gaining momentum over time, the fathers began to confer on Mary significantly more elevated and consequential powers, far beyond conception and birthing.

As early as the sixth century in the Eastern churches of Constantinople, Egypt, Georgia, and Syria, veneration of the Virgin Mary grew as she was revered not only as God-bearer, intercessor, and compassionate maternal figure, but also city protectress, warrior-virgin, and empress. As Byzantine emperors allied themselves more closely with the Christian church, Mary became the poster girl for their own God-given chosenness and power. God, they asserted, was on the side of the Byzantine emperors, as they sponsored Mary's cult throughout the city. In Constantinople, the number and prominence of Mary's feast days increased. Some church rituals and hymns veered toward venerating her in her own right. The rising use of icons (devotional images) of God, Jesus, Mary, and the saints was also a factor in the growing veneration of Mary.

This early wave of devotion became more and more emotional and visceral, sustaining eastern Christians during subsequent seventh- and eighth-century invasions of Persian, Muslim, and Slavic armies. Probably the most striking example occurred when a coalition of Euroasian nomads known as the Avars laid siege to the city of Constantinople in 626. According to an anonymous sermon preached in 627—just one year after the conflict—Mary had been present and powerful during the battle for the city. The preacher seems to have reveled in the story. Scholar Averil Cameron has summarized his sermon as follows, explaining that Mary appeared to the people and soldiers brandishing a sword before the church dedicated to her,

> encouraging the combatants and inspiring them to redden the waters of the imperial city with the blood of Avars and Slavs. She fought as a warrior-maiden . . . and laid low the enemy, women among them. The leader of the Avars saw with his own eyes a veiled lady walking the ramparts; and the Virgin's icons, deployed in procession by the patriarch Sergius . . . stimulated the faith and gratitude of the entire population.[122]

What a vision! The highest church leader, the patriarch of the city, paraded images of Mary throughout the city, holding them high while a battle raged all around him and with the crowd marching behind him.

Another anonymous sermon tells the story of the presence of Mary's robe (complete with milk stains) miraculously rescuing the emperor a few years earlier, in 619, during an earlier conflict. The sermon ends with a prayer, asking Mary ("fount of life, treasury of salvation") to "preserve your grace for your own city, and let not the eyes of men again see the holy church harmed, or this your humble city deserted." The prayer continues, asking Mary to give a peaceful and long reign to "our pious emperors," long life to the holy patriarch, and answers to the prayers of all the people.[123]

Even the anonymous Greek hymn that we looked at in chapter 5—the one that rejoiced that Mary's virgin birth was beyond the comprehension of Greek philosophers—added a new preface that reveled in Mary's role during the battle. After 626, the hymn now began with a speech by the city of Constantinople itself: "I, your city, commemorate the victory festival as a thank-offering to you, Mother of God, our victorious general (or empress), for my cleansing from danger. And you, who have might against which no fight avails, release me from every kind of danger, that I may cry to thee 'Hail, unmarried bride!'"[124] Thus, the postpartum Mary grew in stature and power.

Certainly, the roles of mother, mediator, protector, warrior, and empress are impressive, yet there was yet another role that was even more provocative. It involved Mary's participation in the salvation of humanity. This was a subject that triggered both affirmation and anxiety in early church writings. Many texts presented Mary as powerful, very like Jesus, sometimes even describing her as a co-redeemer of humanity (co-redemptrix). This title had its roots in an early parallel drawn between Mary and Eve (the mother of all humanity). It is found in the writings of our second-century friend, Justin Martyr, in none other than his *Dialogue with Trypho*. In the relevant passage, Justin explains that Eve was an undefiled virgin who gave birth to disobedience and death, while Mary was an undefiled virgin who obediently gave birth to God's victory over both. Importantly, Justin is very clear in this passage that just as Eve was subordinate to Adam in bringing sin to the world, so Mary was subordinate to Jesus in redeeming the world.[125]

The Eve-Mary parallel and its vision of God's salvation of humanity was taken up by Justin's contemporary, the influential church father Irenaeus, who developed it into a fuller theology. It is known as the Christian doctrine of "recapitulation" because it describes God's "re-do" of the fall of humanity. In it, Irenaeus presented Mary's virgin birthing of Jesus as a repetition and reversal of Eve's disobedience, now evolved into obedience, resulting not in death, but in salvation:[126]

> Even though Eve had Adam for a husband, she was still a virgin . . . By disobeying, she became the cause of death for herself and for the whole human race. In the same way, Mary, though she also had a husband, was still a virgin, and by obeying, she became the cause of salvation for herself and for the whole human race . . . The knot of Eve's disobedience was untied by Mary's obedience. What Eve bound through her unbelief, Mary loosed by her faith.[127]

It is hard to overstate the impact of Irenaeus' phrase *causa salutis—the cause of salvation*—in his description of Mary. In the same text, Irenaeus also conferred on Mary the title of "advocate" (defender or mediator), because, through her obedience, Mary redeemed Eve and Eve's sin. Redeemer, advocate, and mediator are functions applied to Jesus and the Holy Spirit in the New Testament. It is true that, just like Justin, Irenaeus was very focused on establishing Jesus as *the* human savior; for instance, in other passages he subordinates Mary's role to Jesus' role as savior. Even so, Irenaeus explicitly afforded to Mary a role, if not *the* role, of redeemer and mediator, someone to whom people could turn to plead their cases before her son and God.[128] Considering that in the apostle Paul's letter to the pastor Timothy, he declares that "there is one God and one mediator between God and Man, Christ Jesus,"[129] we can understand how increasing reliance upon, and veneration of, Mary might cause some church fathers alarm.

Yet both authoritative church leaders and Christian believers continued to see Mary as, at the very least, the most accessible and merciful intercessor or mediator, especially as a mother who would plead for her "children's" salvation. One of the earliest texts that demonstrate this impulse is a third-century prayer from Egyptian Christianity entitled *Sub Tuum Praesidium* ("Under Your Mercy [Care or Help]"). This prayer was probably sung, and it continues to this day as a prayer or hymn in the Coptic, Orthodox, and Roman Catholic churches. Composers, including Mozart and Beethoven, have set it to music across the centuries. It reads as follows: "Under your mercy we take refuge, O Mother of God. Do not reject our supplications in necessity, but deliver us from danger, [O you] alone pure and alone blessed."[130]

This very early prayer to Mary contains a striking echo of the prayer that Jesus taught his disciples to pray to God in the New Testament. Consider that what has become known as "The Lord's Prayer" includes the following lines directed to God himself: "Lead us not into temptation but deliver us from evil." Linguistic echoes are powerful on both the conscious and subconscious levels, even if precise effects will vary. Still, it's clear that, like God, Mary stands between Christian believers and evil.

Similarly, in the fifth century, the French bishop and hymnist Venantius Fortunatus attributed to Mary powers and acts that belong to Jesus alone in the New Testament. In the Gospel of John, Jesus is "the gate" and "the way" to salvation and heaven. In the early creeds of the church, Jesus descends into hell and rescues the souls of those who were sent there before his time on earth, saving them and bringing them to heaven. Yet in Venantius' song, "In Praise of Holy Mary," he describes Mary as "our only remedy," and depicts her as the gate, vehicle, and bridge into heaven, as well as the plunderer of hell and savior of souls imprisoned there:

> Happy are you, who became the ticket, the way, the gate, the vehicle into heaven for the human race, once fallen under hell's dominion. Royal splendor of God, beauty of paradise, glory of the kingdom, receptacle of life, bridge that penetrates into the

> vault of heaven . . . Destroying hell, you bring back captives to their native land; And restore their freedom, after breaking their yokes.[131]

Similarly, in the sixth century, another writer of hymns, Romanos the Melodist, wrote of Mary as the mother of redemption, advocate, and mediator. Romanos was a Jewish convert from Syria who moved to Constantinople and spent his life devoted to Mary. In his *Hymn 2 on Christmas,* Mary speaks directly to Adam and Eve who are inconsolably sad over their fate, and the fate of their children, as sinners.[132] She offers the following promises:

> Cease your laments; I will make myself your advocate in my Son's presence. Meanwhile, no more sadness because I have brought joy to the world. For it is to destroy the kingdom of sorrow that I have come into the world: I, full of grace . . . Then curb your tears; accept me as your mediatrix in the presence of him who was born from me . . . Remain calm; be troubled no longer: I come from him, full of grace.

In this passage, Mary's speech repeatedly echoes Jesus' language as he says farewell to his disciples in the Gospel of John:

- Do not let your hearts be troubled, and do not let them be afraid (John 14:27).
- So you have pain now; but I will see you again, and your hearts will rejoice, and no one will take your joy from you (John 16:22).
- I came from the Father and have come into the world (John 16:28).

For Romanos, Mary claims to come from Jesus, as Jesus came from God. She wishes to make their hearts less troubled, and she promises joy, just as Jesus did. In short, Mary speaks in the same way that Jesus does, comes from where he comes, and promises joy.

The "Hail Mary" prayer that persists to this day carries within it evidence of many of the ideas found in these early prayers, petitions, and promises, as well as their evolution. The beginning lines of the "Hail Mary," written as early as the sixth century, describe the miraculous conception of Jesus ("Hail Mary, full of grace, the Lord is with thee"), reinforcing her role as mother. However, by the fourteenth to fifteenth centuries, new lines had been added, asking for Mary's mediation in sinners' salvation ("Pray for us sinners, now and at the hour of our death"), reflecting her role as mediator. The evolution of the prayer maps the progression of more and more elevated claims about Mary's power.

A Woman Should Know Her Place

From the beginning there were influential early church fathers who challenged the elevation of Mary in the minds of Christians. One method was to merge Mary and her power with the church's power, effectively taking her maternal power from her and relocating it in the church and its male officials. We will look at those texts in the final section of this chapter. The other method was to outright subordinate Mary to church and Christ. For example, Augustine of Hippo in the fourth century engaged in explicit containment of Mary's inflated status. He did this in a sermon in which he played on a metaphor created by the apostle Paul in his letter to the Corinthians. In his letter, Paul described the Corinthian church as "the body of Christ" on earth, made up of many members ("hands," "feet," "eyes") with many gifts (healing, knowledge, prophecy). In his sermon, Augustine insisted:

> Mary is holy. Mary is blessed, but the Church is better than the Virgin Mary. Why? Because Mary is part of the Church, a holy member, an outstanding member, a supereminent member, but a member of the whole body, nonetheless. If she is a member of the whole body, the body is undoubtedly greater than one of its members.[133]

Augustine thus argues that Mary is only a part of Jesus' body (the church), an important one ("supereminent") to be sure, but just a piece, less than the church.

Another fourth-century father, Epiphanius of Salamis, struck a similar note, though he argued Mary was of lesser status than Jesus and God, rather than the church. In his anti-heretical treatise, entitled *Panarion*, Epiphanius makes clear that honoring Mary must only be understood as honoring *Jesus*, in other words, not honoring her in her own right. What prompted this need for clarification? In Epiphanius's crosshairs was a group of Arabian Christians who, he said, worshipped Mary as a goddess. Accordingly, he wrote:

> Yes, Mary's body was holy, but it was not God. Yes, the Virgin was surely a virgin and worthy of honor; however, she was not given us for us to adore her. She herself adored him who was born of her flesh, having descended from heaven and from the bosom of the Father.[134]

These fourth-century texts suggest that some Christians were elevating, even worshipping, Mary. No doubt, some were influenced by forms of goddess worship that surrounded the early Christian movement. Indeed, some scholars argue that early church fathers may have added to Mary's powers, assigning to her already existing mother goddess roles and images precisely because they would have been familiar and possibly compelling to Pagan goddess worshippers of that time. Long-standing scholarship points to material evidence, such as statues of Mary holding Jesus on her lap that closely mirrored statues of the Egyptian goddess Isis with her son Horus on her lap. They also note that the council of bishops that declared Mary the mother of God took place in Ephesus, a center of devotion to the goddess Artemis, who was also understood as both virgin and mother goddess.

These connections make sense when you consider that the church's depictions of Mary, from humble, obedient maid to warrior-empress to mother of a god, were increasingly communicated within complicated intercultural settings, amongst people from all across the Mediterranean. The original, very small Jewish sect of Jesus followers was becoming a multicultural movement filled with people from very different philosophical and religious backgrounds. It is important, in my view, to appreciate that this kind of "translation" often requires sharing religious teachings *using listeners' words and ideas,* so that they may begin to make connections with what they already know. Only then can the translator go on to explain how the teachings are different than more familiar ideas. On this more sympathetic view, sharing religious beliefs and practices is not always a case of imposition on, or cynical manipulation of, the beliefs and practices of those being approached. It is a case of trying hard to be understood. However, even if this were the case—*and this is the point here*—what listeners actually understand, what actually moves and resonates within them in such translations, is impossible to control. It is precisely this lack of control that moved the church fathers from acts of translation to acts of regulation and indoctrination. We see this clearly demonstrated in the passages from Augustine and Epiphanius above.

The diverse, multicultural nature of Christianity today, the largest of the global religions, is not so very different than that of the early Christian movement. Similar "translational" issues are still in play. No surprise, then, that the regulation of doctrines persists in, for instance, official papal pronouncements about Mary. Nor should it surprise us that such doctrines continue to effectively merge Mary with her son, thus erasing any possibility that she might be interpreted as playing an independent or equal role in redemption.

For example, the 1964 Vatican II document entitled "Light of the Nations" presents official doctrine on what the church is and has been, and, among other dogmatic concerns, a chapter on Marian doctrine. In that chapter, Mary is said to occupy "a place in the Church which is *the highest after Christ* and yet very close to us."[135] The doctrine asserts that God "*used her* not merely in a passive way, but as freely *cooperating* in the work of human salvation through faith and obedience."[136] Then, most interestingly to me—because it relates to my discussion in chapter 5 on the cannibalizing of Mary's flesh—the document moves to a veritable *merging of Mary into* Jesus' death on the cross and its salvific effects:

> After this manner the Blessed Virgin advanced in her pilgrimage of faith, and faithfully persevered in her union with her Son unto the cross, where she stood, in keeping with the divine plan, grieving exceedingly with her only begotten Son, uniting herself with a maternal heart with His sacrifice, and lovingly consenting to the immolation of this Victim which she herself had brought forth.[137]

Thus, not only in gestation and childbearing, but in Jesus' death, Mary's heart and being are incorporated into Jesus' dying flesh and the redemption it wrought. This last passage is widely referred to as the "co-redemptrix paragraph," although Pope Paul VI did not use that term anywhere in the document.

This reticence of Pope Paul VI notably contrasts with later pronouncements by Pope John Paul II, who also favored the theme of Mary's perfect union with Jesus but *did* use the title co-redemptrix to refer to Mary. In his 1987 *Mother of the Redeemer*, John Paul wrote of Mary's role in salvation, and also as mother and mediator. The document begins: "The Mother of the Redeemer has a precise place in the plan of salvation."[138] Yet, even as John Paul advises special veneration of, and devotion to, Mary, he remains intent on placing that veneration within the context of the "perfect union" of Mary and Jesus in his salvific death:

> Through this faith Mary is perfectly united with Christ in his self-emptying . . . At the foot of the Cross Mary shares through faith in the shocking mystery of this self-emptying. This is perhaps the deepest "kenosis" in faith in human history . . . the Mother shares in the death of her Son, in His redeeming death.[139]

Under the cross, Mary faithfully "empties herself" (this is the meaning of the Greek word *kenosis*) just as Jesus emptied himself, disappearing into his act of redemption. Mary's suffering watching Jesus die is also a "death" that "shares" in the redemptive act. The verbs used in this formulation of Mary's suffering, and other formulations like it, are fascinating: "uniting," "sharing," "joining," "co-operating" in redemption, yet not herself redeeming. Thus, Mary is subsumed *into* her son in life and death. This containment of Mary testifies to her continued suspension between power and subordination.

So, the story of Mary is also suspended between her own being, her own presence, and her son's. As recently as 1993, Mark Miravalle, a professor of theology at Franciscan University of Steubenville, founded a lay organization known as "The Voice of the People for Mary Mediatrix." This group is supported by some eight million Catholics, including eight hundred bishops, who seek to have a fifth Marian dogma added to the church's official doctrine, naming Mary "Co-redemptrix, Mediatrix of All Graces, and Advocate." This is not a fringe group, though it has its opponents. Mother Teresa supported the fifth dogma and Pope Francis may not use the title "co-redemptrix," but he continues to speak of Mary's "yes" as "a central moment in salvation history." Doubtless, the subordination of Mary to Jesus in the redemption of humanity is *not* in question, but the popular need to turn to Mary in life's darkest moments and seek deliverance is not going anywhere.

FAREWELL TO THE MOTHERS' FLESH: HAIL, HOLY MOTHER CHURCH

The early diversity of the Christian movement and the indoctrinating response of the early church to that diversity are echoed in today's Marian debates. Both bring us back to the heart of the matter and to the question with which we began: who are the chosen and the saved and *how did they become so*? We have studied the ways in which motherhood has been used to define and distinguish peoples: Israelites, Ishmaelites, Ammonites, Moabites, Jews, Pagans, and Christians.

In this final section, I will map the early church's co-optation of Mary's motherhood, her breasts, her womb, and her delivery of the savior (and thereby salvation) to the people of God. We will look at texts that assign the ability to birth and save new sons of God, not to any human mother, but to the church alone as the mother of the saved (chosen). The metaphor that described the church as "mother of the faithful" enabled early Christians to claim an identity, a spiritual "family," and an inheritance, above and beyond all those around them. The metaphors of conception, pregnancy, birthing, and lactation were once again linked to peoplehood, just as they were in the Hebrew Bible mother-stories. Now, however, the people-defining power of mothers was co-opted to legitimize not only Christian identity, but also the church's authority and the necessary nurture that its teachings provided to its "children."

As early as the second century, the church fathers Irenaeus and Clement of Alexandria were using maternal and kinship metaphors in ways that relocated salvific power from biblical mothers to God and the church.[140] Two examples from their writings will suffice to demonstrate the way in which metaphors of the maternal breast and breast milk worked to authorize the emerging church and its doctrines over and against "heretical" versions of Christianity, and to define orthodox Christians as "the saved." In both cases, the authors used as their springboard a passage from a letter that the apostle Paul wrote to the Corinthians.

In his letter, Paul was trying to bring the Corinthian church members back to the original teachings he had shared with them when he visited among them. Since then, they had become divided, with a group of them promoting human spiritual wisdom as the path to salvation. In 1 Corinthians 2:1–2, 4–5, Paul writes about the foolishness of human wisdom, when compared to God's power:

> When I came to you, brothers and sisters, I did not come proclaiming the mystery of God to you in lofty words or wisdom. For I decided to teach nothing among you except Jesus Christ, and him crucified . . . My speech and my proclamation were not with plausible words of wisdom, but with a demonstration of the Spirit and of power, so that your faith might rest not on human wisdom but on the power of God.

Paul goes on to write about "God's wisdom, secret and hidden," and to explain that it takes time for *infant* (new) Christians to be able to speak of that wisdom. One had to be "taught by the Spirit," as *mature* Christians like himself had been taught. It is at this point that the passage that proved inspiring to Irenaeus and Clement of Alexandria appears. At 1 Corinthians 3:1–3, Paul tells the Corinthians,

> And so, brothers and sisters, I could not speak to you as spiritual people, but rather as people of the flesh, *as infants in Christ. I fed you with milk*, not solid food, for you were not ready for solid food. Even now you are still not ready, for you are still of the flesh.

Using this metaphor as a springboard, Irenaeus and Clement used Paul's breast milk metaphors to restore dignity to belief in the Christian gospel. Why dignity? The problem was that a messiah's death on a cross, which Paul had defined as God's wisdom and power in 1 Corinthians, was considered ridiculous by second-century philosophers and spiritual wisdom seekers. The intellectual and spiritual superiority of such a belief had to be established, and "the milk of the Spirit" and the secret, superior wisdom it imparted was just the ticket.

Beyond this concern, however, Irenaeus and Clement went further, presenting the church itself and its teachings as the source of "God's milk," making all "foolish" Christians brothers and sisters, heirs to the most powerful of spiritual wisdoms, bonded to each other as family, identified as saved. The insertion of the church into the process of salvation was key. So, Irenaeus would write of divine milk provided to humanity so that they, "nourished, as it were, by the breast of [Jesus'] flesh and habituated through such lactation, can grow to 'eat and drink' the Word of God."[141] As we shall see below, these breasts and this lactation become identified with church doctrine.

Reinforcing the same metaphors, Clement of Alexandria wrote:

> This food is the milk of the Father, by which alone we infants are nursed. Thus the Beloved himself, the Word, is also our food, the one who poured out his blood on our behalf to save humanity. Because of the Word we who believed in God escape to the "care-banishing breasts" of the Father, the Word. The Father alone, however, as is fitting, supplies us infants with the milk of love—and only these are truly satisfied; whoever suckles at this breast.[142]

Still, there is more. Indeed, as we recall and map the deep and persistent connection between the mothers' bodies and the defining of peoples who are favored by God over all others, we should almost expect what comes next. Clement goes on to explain that the grace, illumination, regeneration, and perfection that this spiritual nourishment produces are for Christians, and not "the ancient race" that was "perverse and hard-hearted."[143] "The ancient, hard-hearted race" is none other than the ancient Hebrews and, by extension, their first-century descendants, from whom these fathers intended to distance themselves and their congregations at all costs. So it is that the breast-feeding virgin mother had to be understood as one not with her Jewish forebears, but rather with God the Father, the Word, the Holy Spirit, and, most importantly, with the church itself. They all had to be made, "one and the same everywhere." Together, they were the progenitors of perfected Christians: "O mystic marvel! The universal Father is one, and one the universal Word; and the Holy Spirit is one and the same everywhere, and one is the only virgin mother. I love to call her the Church."[144]

Once again, we encounter a maternal continuum, very like those we explored in chapter 3, in *Odes of Solomon* and *Sybilline Oracles*. Only now the continuum extends to "Holy Mother Church," birthing and feeding all newborn Christians. Clement concludes his text explaining that, "This mother," the church, "calling her children to her, nurses them with holy milk."[145]

In sum, we are here witness to the metaphor of God's breast-feeding being used to distinguish Christian sons of God from the ancient Hebrews, who, after all, had only been promised ordinary milk and honey, had only been fed with mere matriarchal milk. The claim is not one of continuity but rupture, separation, disavowal. Clement is quite clear about this: "We are enjoined to cast off the old and carnal corruption, as also the old nutriment, receiving in exchange another new regimen, that of Christ."[146]

This cooptation of the maternal to authorize the still-nascent church and her sons as the true elect became extremely popular. In the third century, Hippolytus described the Old and New Testaments as breasts: "Blessing of *breasts: or rather the two Testaments*, from which came forth the preaching that announced the future appearance of the Word in the world; breasts *with which he [the Word/Jesus] nurses and feeds us*, presenting us to God as sons."[147]

In the fourth and fifth centuries, the use of maternal metaphors extended beyond the equating of breast milk with church doctrines; it now co-opted an even more powerful part of Mary's body: her womb and its life-giving power. For just one of many examples, our old friend, Ephrem of Syria, who was so devoted to Mary, used womb imagery to describe the church's baptismal rites. For Ephrem, it is the Holy Spirit, priests, baptismal fonts, and altars who give birth to, and suckle, new sons of God:

> They [converts to Christianity] go down sordid with sin,
> they go up pure like children,
> for *baptism is a second womb* for them.
> *Rebirth in the font* rejuvenates the old, as the river rejuvenated Naaman.
> O womb that gives birth without pangs to the children of the kingdom!
> The priesthood ministers to this womb as it gives birth;
> anointing precedes it, the Holy Spirit hovers over its streams,
> a crown of Levites surrounds it, the chief priest is its minister,
> the angels rejoice at the lost who in it are found.
> Once this womb has given birth, *the altar suckles and nurtures them*:
> her children eat straight away, not milk, but perfect bread![148]

That "a crown of Levites" [Israelite priests] surrounds the womb/baptismal font of the church points both to the original Hebrew Bible focus on motherhood, as well as the transformation that the divine-maternal womb has undergone. It is not the matriarchs now, but rather priests that birth new sons of God. The mothers' wombs are now baptismal fonts. Their breasts are altars. Their milk is dispensed in the communion meal at the altar; it has become Jesus' flesh, sacrificed for all on the cross. Leo the Great in the fifth century summed it all up neatly in a sermon he preached: "The water of baptism is like the virginal womb . . . By the Spirit, Christ is born from the body of his *unsullied Mother*; by this same Spirit, the Christian is reborn from the womb of *holy Church*."[149]

I am hopeful that what resonates within you as you read this chapter is just how closely these legitimizing maternal metaphors used by the church, to define itself as central to salvation and better than its Jewish roots, resemble the interventions and life-giving power of the God of the Hebrew Bible when God opened the matriarchs' wombs to produce chosen sons of the promise. This persistent ill-conceived logic, however reassuringly and softly its metaphors may weave their web, still sets apart a people, now a church, as the true sons of God. The mothers' wombs, their mode of conception, and their delivery of sons have been appropriated and become a fully disembodied mother creating new elect children. The procreating God-of-the-Womb is now Jesus and his blood; he still generates the chosen people, now with his wife, the church. Like the Hebrew Bible God, he is still the agent and enforcer of righteousness and redemption. And the maternal womb, its procreative power now fully co-opted by a human institution, endures as a defenseless tool of legitimation.

III

EPILOGUE

Love, Hate, and Legacies

In my family of origin, my parents would regularly tell my sisters and me that we were "special." It became increasingly clear over time that, by this, they did not mean "to them," or "just wonderful," they meant "better." It also did not take me long to figure out that we were no more special than any other family who saw themselves as special. In fact, we were a hurting, troubled, and violent family. Even in that reality, we were not unusual.

My country also considers itself special. American exceptionalism argues that the United States stands alone as a bastion of liberty, equality, and democracy. It has taken Americans far too long to recognize that we are not as exceptional as we believe; instead, we are a hurting, troubled, and violent nation. Our culture is riddled—shot through—with the repercussions of African American slavery, the disempowerment of women, deep and abiding racism, economic injustice, and hatred of sexual minorities. Yes, we do represent the best of hopes: a uniquely pluralistic promise, with laws that seek to protect freedoms and promote justice. Unfortunately, in our execution of those hopes, we are failing.

In—as I write—these dog days of the COVID-19 pandemic, it could not be clearer how we suffer from an overemphasis on our "rights," and woeful neglect of our "responsibilities" to each other. We are individualists, not collectivists; we compete in a ruthless political and economic oligarchy; we do not trust each other. Worst of all, our most brilliant prophetic voices, who could be the conscience of our culture, are being drowned out in a cacophony of spin and "alternative facts," voices such as Cornel West (*Race Matters*), Barbara Ehrenreich (*Nickled and Dimed*), Martha Nussbaum (*Sex and Social Justice*), Noam Chomsky (*Requiem for the American Dream*), Mary Warnock (*Question of Life*), and Ta-Nehisi Coates (*Between the World and Me*).

I have shared in this book how biblical ideals of motherhood and family, and their interpretation over time, have been used to breed disavowal, denunciation, and violence amongst Jews, Christians, and all those who are perceived to be "Other." I have argued that the cost of such biblical ideals, and the stories that birthed them, to women, to sexual psychology, and to racial and ethnic understanding is pervasive, often unconscious, and deeply saddening. How does this happen? Where are such messages found? We might consider the following somewhat random list:

- Jerry Falwell's popularization of the 1977 Christian catchphrase, "Adam and Steve."
- Herman Melville's hero in *Moby-Dick*: "Call me Ishmael."
- Madonna's 1984 hit single: "Like a Virgin."
- All those mass-produced portraits of Warner Sallman's blond-haired, blue-eyed "Euro-Jesus" with which I grew up (500 million copies sold).
- The *Left Behind* novels by Tim LaHaye and Jerry B. Jenkins,which my students read, now a multimedia franchise, and their central conflict between foxhole Christian converts and the "global community."

There are many more examples. "The biblical" permeates Western culture. My nephew's name is Noah. My mother's was Mary. My students are Rachel, Sarah, Abraham, and David. I have yet to meet a Jezebel, though I would like to, if only to offer solidarity. The Bible is alive in the popular mind. It informs the endless and superficial moralizing of mainstream media.

The underlying messages in the examples I have chosen above involve condemnation, exile, white co-optation of Israelite identity, dangerous female sexuality, and the demonization of non-Christians. All of these are themes that we have explored in the biblical mother-stories. Heterosexual love and the command to bear children is behind the condemnation of gay men as unnatural: God made Adam and Eve, not Adam and Steve. Melville's Ishmael is an exiled son who survives as a witness to Captain Ahab's fixation on the white whale. He wanders over the sea, just as Hagar and her son wandered in the desert because of Abraham's fixation on God's promise, and he too survives. (I cannot help but note here that Melville's Ishmael is not saved by God, as the biblical Ishmael was, but by a ship named . . . Rachel!) The desexualization of women and mothers is gleefully mocked in Madonna's persona and song, "Like a Virgin," even more aggressively in its accompanying music video. The rejection of neighboring peoples, even those with common origins and history, is reinforced and encouraged in readers of the *Left Behind* series, as it popularizes toxic division and distrust of international cooperation and common cause.

Regarding individual readers' consumption of such "interpretations" in popular culture—and I speak now to women—we can only try to raise our consciousness as to their effects. There are so many aspects of the mothers' stories that vividly call to mind realities that many women continue to experience today. I am thinking of the skepticism leveled at us as mothers, as leaders, as wives, of our sexualities and our desire; the considerable pressure to bear children; the programmed fear and grief internalized by childless wives and aging single women whose "biological clocks are ticking"; the expectation that our loyalties should be to men, not women; our economic disadvantage, indeed, vulnerability; our absence from, or marginal status in, our own history; male anticipation and fear of our deceitfulness, unfaithfulness, "ball-breaking," or independence (choose whatever stereotype you like); and perhaps worst of all, the setting of us, one against the other, in competition for husbands, material support, children, and social standing.

I know that not all women see their lives in this way, but these cultural messages are endemic and resilient, and they play out in many women's day-to-day lives. I know that there are good men, happy marriages, and I myself have known the joy of mothering daughters. Yet, I have also seen the anguish and anger of women who either cannot or do not wish to have children. The weight of social expectations, invasive personal questions, pity, and judgement lies heavy on them.

Such powerful cultural messages affect men and women, and they bear an intimate relationship to the biblical mother-stories, where women were also scrutinized, judged, and valued primarily as mothers. It is true that our gendered experiences today exist in a time and culture far removed from the biblical world of ancient Israel. In ancient Israel, having many children was essential to the survival of nuclear and/or extended families. Children helped shoulder the significant labor required in an agricultural economy. Yet childhood death rates were high, as were women's deaths in childbirth, making the need for continued sexual reproduction, and more than one wife, even higher. Today's situation is radically different, due to all kinds of factors, from overpopulation to the climate crisis. The birth rate in the US is at a historic low, well below "replacement levels." The BBC recently reported a "'jaw-dropping' global crash in children being born."[150] Wars, global warming, climate refugees, increased migration, economic inequality, food insecurity, all increase widespread apprehension that having children is not advisable or responsible. Yet, even in such an environment, the cultural cost of not having children for many women continues to be levied against them—which should give us pause. Yes, history matters. Lifestyles and challenges change, but cultural messages are resilient. Certainly, messages about gender have proven to be.

Can we lay all gender issues at the feet of the biblical authors? Of course not. Can we claim a direct influence of the Bible on Western culture today? Of course. Yes, *and*, it is in the transmission across time that the workings of that influence become most clear. There have been many hands set to that work, many minds in many times and places that have produced that web of influence, creating variations on persistent themes that rise and fall over time. That is why I have chosen to describe how the mother-stories have been read and transmitted, what has been changed, and what has endured.

Here is what I know. Stories open eyes and speak to hearts. They encourage identification with their characters and what happens to them. Indeed, many scholars agree that such identification and imitation have always been the purpose of biblical stories, for good or ill. The mother-stories recalled in this chapter resonate within me and cause me no small amount of grief. It is hard to read the story of Sarah and Hagar, or of Leah and Rachel, and not recognize the all too familiar story of rivalry between women competing with one another for the same man. These days, such stories often feature a sexually aggressive single woman who is out to take a husband from a married woman, but often the reality is not so black and white, and the purportedly "sexually aggressive" single woman is not the monster we have been primed to see. I have seen women express moral outrage and even make violent threats aimed at "the other woman," with no attention paid to their husband's actions or responsibility. When one woman's ethnicity or culture is contrasted with another's, the door is further opened to racialized as well as sexualized stereotypes and antagonisms. The loss of solidarity and mutual support among women is painful. It weakens all women.

It is important to recognize that this story of competition between women—then and now—was and is a product of the economic vulnerability and political powerlessness that women have endured. It does not prove some sort of "natural" animosity or enmity between women. In ancient Israel, women had no social or economic status or security and were utterly dependent on men for their survival, even though there were laws in place to protect the poor, widows, orphans, and strangers. Today, women have made great progress in becoming more independent economically, though this varies by geography, ethnicity, and age. Nevertheless, gendered economic disparities are well-documented even in the so-called developed countries. Encountering the stories of Sarah and Hagar, or Leah and Rachel, can imprint on our hearts the ways that real and unequal material conditions produce the stories we tell about ethnic and gender relations. For many women, part of reading and hearing such stories is to struggle against internalizing such negative depictions of our relationships to each other, and to pay attention, again, to ways that we are dependent on men, or not.

As for the ignorance, fear, and hostility between "races" and ethnicities that continue in America today, it is obvious that we are in crisis and have been for a very long time. Our exploration in this book has, I hope, demonstrated ways in which biblical echoes of the mother-stories are not helping. Indeed, to make this observation clearer, I would like to provide an example of how those echoes reverberate and become more and more distorted.

In the eighteenth and nineteenth centuries, a belief system known as "Anglo-Israelism" gained momentum in England. It argued that the English were the true Israel (the ten lost tribes)[151] and that God's special covenant was with the Anglo-Saxons or Germanic peoples. These ideas hit America in the early twentieth century, embraced and promoted by Henry Ford (founder of the Ford Motor Company, hardly a marginal figure, rather a successful and influential leader within the American mainstream).[152] Ford arranged for the publication of the now-famous manifesto entitled *Protocols of the Elders of Zion*, a turn-of-the-century hoax, originally penned by a czarist official, popular in Russia, Poland, England, and France. It was translated into English in 1920 and sent to *The Dearborn Independent*, in which Ford's protégé William J. Cameron, an adherent of Anglo-Israelism, published a series of articles featuring its main argument that successful Jews were planning to secretly take over the world.[153]

At the same time (1930s–1940s), Anglo-Israelism developed into a worldview known as "Christian Identity" in America. Among its tenets was a narrative that "white Christians would wage a great battle on the side of God against Satan, the Jews, and people of color" at the end of the world.[154] Subsequently, they would win and reign with Christ for a thousand years.

You will probably not, at this point, be surprised that race and ethnicity were interjected into this narrative through a mother-story. Eve and Satan (the serpent in the garden of Eden) gave birth to Cain, and thereby to all Jews and people of color, all of whom hate white people. Eve and Adam gave birth to the white race. Adam was a white man (!); the white nations are thus his and Eve's offspring. It seems we are *not* all brothers and sisters after all. We are *not* all one body of Christ.

Thus, the righteous and the wicked, the saved and the damned, are defined racially. White, Anglo-Saxon, Germanic peoples are the true, biological "children of Israel." They must be kept pure and separated from the world, not least because they are being persecuted by non-whites and the federal government. Luckily, Jesus is coming back any minute and the battle will begin.[155] So, Proud (white) Boys, *stand back and stand by*.

Some have written off such thinking in the past as fringe, extremist, and not representative of our country. Surely now, though, the existence and influence of such ideas in mainstream America is clearer than ever before, in the midst of America's "reckoning with race" and its "#MeToo" movement; in the face of endless police shootings of black citizens and white nationalist rallies like that held in Charlottesville, Virginia in 2017 that feature chants like "Jews will not replace us!" and threats to "Jewish communists" and "criminal niggers"; and in the aftermaths of domestic terrorism and mass shootings aimed at women (Oregon, Florida),[156] Jews (Pittsburgh),[157] and Hispanic immigrants (El Paso).[158]

Links to motherhood and family are not obscure or difficult to find in such racist agendas. From Eve and the serpent to imagined threats to the white race, mothers and family stand front and center. Take, for instance, the white supremacist belief that whites must not intermarry and dilute the chosen race (as the children of Cain—the Jews—did), or the command that white Christians must have as many children as possible with white wives, producing saved Christian sons and daughters for the battle ahead. White mothers and their children are also seen as useful on a PR level, because they create the illusion that white supremacy is benign, thereby further facilitating its mainstreaming. Case studies have shown that white mothers have been seduced into these groups by promises of safety and opportunity for their children. Seward Darby, author of *Sisters in Hate*, spent time with three white women immersed in the white nationalist movement. She reports how the promise of safety is leveraged by such women, for instance, "It's not that I hate Black people, I just want the best for my own children."[159]

"The best for my children." Well, who can argue with that? And what is best for children? For families? For single or married, happily childless neighbors? For beautiful, sexual, loving human bodies? Do the Jewish-Christian stories of the Bible answer these questions in ways that breed love, connection, and justice? These are hard questions. We have explored some answers in this book. Yet, as we have learned, the conversation will inevitably continue.

To conclude, then, I will leave you with a beautiful poem by the writer and feminist Audre Lorde, a self-proclaimed "black, lesbian, mother, warrior, poet." This poem, "Black Mother Woman," is one I have returned to over and over again while writing this book. In it, Lorde is talking to her mother. As I read it now, in this context, I wonder if it is possible to "interpret" the biblical mothers in new ways, wherever and in whatever cultural medium we encounter them. How will we "read" them? What will we share about them? Is there a "core of love"? Or only denial?

I cannot recall you gentle
yet through your heavy love
I have become

an image of your once-delicate flesh
split with deceitful longings.
When strangers come and compliment me
your aged spirit takes a bow
jingling with pride
but once you hid that secret
in the center of your fury
hanging me
with deep breasts and wiry hair
your own split flesh
and long-suffering eyes
buried in myths of little worth.
But I have peeled away your anger
down to its core of love
and look mother
I am a dark temple
where your true spirit rises
beautiful tough as chestnut
stanchion against nightmares of weakness
and if my eyes conceal
a squadron of conflicting rebellions
I learned from you
to define myself through your denials.[160]

Endnotes

CHAPTER 1

1. For one good example of Augustine's views on sex, marriage, and sin, I suggest his book *Of Marriage and Concupiscence*, which was written about 420–21 CE.

2. Eve is, of course, the first mother in the Bible. However, she is the mother of all humanity and not just one select group, such as Israel, the chosen people, or Christians who are saved. Since this book is about how maternal bodies are used to define chosen or "saved" status and differentiate those who have it from "Others," I will not be writing about Eve. In a later section, however, I will discuss how later writers used Eve to define Mary (through contrasting them).

3. There are many resources that provide statistics and analyses of the global prevalence of incest today. For example, see the 2004 World Health Organization report, "WHO, Child sexual abuse: a silent health emergency."

4. Stiebert, *Fathers and Daughters*, 165.

5. Genesis 9 provides a backstory to this later hatred of the Canaanites. Ham was one of the three sons of Noah who survived the flood on the ark. Canaan was Ham's son and Noah's grandson. In Genesis 9, the family is back on dry land and Noah has planted a vineyard. He proceeds to get drunk and fall asleep. Ham then "sees his father's nakedness." We know by looking at lots of other biblical passages where this phrase is used that it often means "have intercourse with." This explains why Shem and Japheth will not look at Noah asleep and why Noah "knows what Ham has *done* to him" and curses him, his son Canaan, and their descendants. This story of father-son incest, clearly condemned in the Hebrew Bible, produces the condemnation of the Canaanites and, ironically, a vigorous insistence on endogamy in later texts like *Jubilees*. The further implications of Genesis 9 for our own current divisions and hatreds are multiple: Ham is understood by church fathers in the first centuries of the church as dark-skinned, black. This interpretation bred ongoing racial hatred and ideologies of white supremacy that had done untold damage. Ham's incest with his father has also served through the centuries as a foundational passage for the religious rejection of homosexual relationships.

CHAPTER 2

6. Kara-Ivanov Kaniel, "Myth of the Messianic Mother," 78.

CHAPTER 3

7. Kristeva, "Stabat Mater," 145.

8. Chrysostom, *Adv. Jud. [Against the Jews]* 2. While much of Chrysostom's attention is focused on Jewish law, rituals, and festivals, he also engages in ethnic slurs, calling Jews "abominable and lawless and murderous and enemies of God." The history of the violent legacies of such early Christian anti-Jewish invective is too big a subject to broach in this project. It has been written about by many scholars better versed in the topic. One of the most compelling and readable is James Carroll's *Constantine's Sword*.

9. Roncace and Whitehead. "Reading the Religious Romance," 113–14.

10. Acts 5:15; Ps 91:4; Gen 2; and Exod 40:15 .

11. Sebastian Brock, a respected scholar of Syriac Christianity, offers a detailed catalogue of genealogies of the Virgin Mary that establish her Davidic lineage in Brock, "Genealogy of the Virgin Mary in Sinai Syr. 16." The *First Gospel of James*, a noncanonical Gospel of the second century, is the first to assign Mary Davidic lineage by identifying her parents as Joachim and Anna, who are of the tribes of Judah and Levi, respectively. Other Greek texts in the Syriac tradition argue that Mary and her husband Joseph descended from different sons of Eleazar, also of the Davidic line. These texts no doubt aimed to answer questions about Jesus' place in the Davidic line, since in the Gospel of Matthew only Joseph belongs to that line, and not Mary, and yet Joseph does not physically father Jesus. Note how physical, biological reproduction remains definitive in the minds of early Christians, in spite of new ideologies of spiritual (re) birth in Christ.

12. These representative quotes are from Chadwick, "Reflections," 246.

13. Translation by Drijvers, "19th Ode of Solomon," 339–40.

14. Corrington, "Milk of Salvation," 410.

15. *Odes Sol.* 8:13–14 (*OTP* 2:742).

16. If you wish to see the original Hebrew Bible texts in which these phrases and ideas can be found, go to Isaiah 11:1, Psalm 118:22, and Isaiah 28:16. Moses was of course the great liberating prophet who freed Israel from its enslavement in Egypt. Isaiah 11 is a prophecy of the coming messiah. Its description of "a shoot" coming out from the house of Jesse, and "a branch" growing out of Jesse's roots, becomes "a staff of David" here. In Psalm 118, the victories of the messiah are celebrated. The "one who comes in the name of the LORD" is referred to as "the stone that the builders rejected," which has now "become the chief cornerstone." Isaiah 28 contains a promise from God that the wayward Israelites can find their way back to him. To help them, God says, "See, I am laying in Zion a foundation stone, a tested stone, a precious cornerstone, a sure foundation." In Oracle 8, this stone is Jesus.

17. *Sib. Or.* 8.264–70 (*OTP* 1:424)

18. This mix of the spiritual and the physical is also present in the description of Jesus, who is progressively described as word, breath, flesh, mortal form, and boy.

19. *Sib. Or.* 8.460–72 (*OTP* 1:428).

20. If you are interested in this tradition of Jesus-as-angel, read Hannah, *Michael and Christ*. Here I am focusing on his discussion on pages 171–96 of that book. His discussion in the book as a whole ranges across texts such as *Testament of Solomon*, *Revelations of Elchasai*, *Shepherd of Hermas*, *Gospel of the Hebrews*, and more. Another good book to explore is Grillmeier, *Christ in Christian Tradition*, 38–68. He offers a broad analysis of second century Jewish-Christian texts and their Christologies. His overview covers the Old Testament Apocrypha (where they appear to be Jewish-Christian or Christian revisions) as well as New Testament Apocrypha and liturgical, moral, ascetical, and catechetical texts. Here I am using his analysis in pages 46–49 of that book.

21. In this sermon, Cyril indicates that he got the account from "the Gospel of the Hebrews." The scholarly reconstruction of this "gospel" out of fragmentary quotes from the Fathers is ongoing. It is most often dated to the first half of the second century CE which would make it roughly contemporary to the *Sibylline Oracles*. I cite here a description of Jesus' conception that Cyril of Jerusalem offered in a fourth-century sermon and which he then roundly denounced as heretical. Many argue that the "Coptic Cyril fragment" does not belong in a reconstructed Gospel of the Hebrews.

22. Cyril of Jerusalem, *Catechesis* 12.32; PG 33: 765 B).

23. *Ep. Apos.* 14 (*NT Apoc.*, 1:199).

24. *Sib. Or.* 8.272 (*OTP* 1:424).

25. *Sib. Or.* 8.324–36 (*OTP* 1:425).

26. *Sib. Or.* 8.483–84 (*OTP* 1:429).

CONCLUSION TO PART 1

27. Angier, "For Motherly X Chromosome, Gender Is Only the Beginning," para. 2.

CHAPTER 4

28. Moraga and Anzaldúa, *This Bridge Called My Back*.

29. Only 2 Kings 4 bears a slight resemblance: the childless Shunammite woman, like Sarah, has an old husband. Like Sarah, she doubts Elisha's promise that she will have a child, but she does not laugh; she begs him not to trick her, and her doubt is momentary.

30. Rashi, *Gen.* 18.12.1–2.

31. Radak, *Gen.* 18:2.

32. Radak, *Gen.* 18.12.1–15.2

33. Rashi, *Gen.* 25.19.2.

34. *b. Yebam.* 64a–64b.

35. *b. Sanh.* 69b.

36. *Gen. Rab.*, *R. Bachya*, *Akeidat Yitzchak*, and more.

37. *R. Bachya* Gen 19:30.2. This is a fourteenth-century Spanish commentary written by Rabbi Bachya ben Asher, 1255–1340.

38. *Tur HaArokh* is a commentary on the Torah, written by Rabbi Jacob ben Asher (c. 1269–c. 1343).

39. Radak, *Gen.* 19.31.2; *Tur HaArokh* Gen. 19.30, Gen. 19.30.1.

40. Rashi, *Gen.* 19.36.1; 19.33.1.

41. *R. Bachya* Gen. 19.33.1.

42. *Tur HaArokh* Gen. 19.37.1.

43. Cf. *R. Bachya* Gen. 19.30.2. By giving birth to Ruth, the Moabitess, and Naamah, the Ammonite wife of King Solomon's son, "both of Lot's daughters acquired a share in the Kingdom of David."

44. *Gen. Rab.* 51.8.

45. My logic here parallels arguments in Kara-Ivanov Kaniel, "Myth of the Messianic Mother."

46. Rashi, *Gen.* 19.33.2.

47. Rashi, *Gen.* 19.33.3; *Gen. Rab.* 51.9.

48. Radak, *Gen.* 19.32.2; 19:33.2.

49. *Tur HaArokh* Gen. 19:32.1.

50. *Tur HaArokh* Gen. 19:32.1.

51. Talmudic texts: recall that the rabbis collected centuries of their biblical commentaries from the second to sixth centuries in the Jerusalem and Babylonian Talmuds.

52. *b. Sanh.* 109b.9.

53. *Pirqe R. El.* 25.8.

54. *Sep. HaYashar*, 5.

55. There are so many cultural expressions of these inherited ideals that it would take a book in itself to "prove" the resilience of the messages we are exploring in the ongoing influence of the biblical mothers. One article that I have found particularly compelling comes out of a study by a professor of sociology, Beth Montemurro, in which she studied conceptions of mothers in Western culture, particularly of mothers' sexuality. (Montemurro and Siefken, "MILFS and Matrons.") Montemurro and her research assistant, Siefken, interviewed fifty-five women aged twenty to forty-nine, the majority of whom were heterosexual. They were asked about how they viewed their mothers as well as their own experiences as mothers. One question posed was "What is your image of a mother's sexuality? Do you think women who are mothers should show their sexuality in a way that is different from women who are not mothers?" One response (which was representative of many in the study) reads as follows: "You're not supposed to dress [sexually] if you're a mom. What kind of image is that putting forth? It may not be fair to the other part of you who may still feel like an unmarried or newly married woman, but you never know." Another: "Being at things with my kids and all, you do have these moms that are like hot mammas or whatever. And I just think it's inappropriate sometimes, you do have children . . . You're supposed to be an example to your children." I include these examples, instead of examples of cultural messaging (ads, self-help books, films), to emphasize the *reception* of such ideals. The ideals that emerge out of the biblical traditions continue to be received and internalized by women *and* men.

56. The literary and historical background I present in this section comes partly from Malkiel, "Manipulating Virginity," and Kara-Ivanov Kaniel, "Myth of the Messianic Mother."

57. There are an increasing number of studies on Babylonian rabbinic writings that focus on rabbinic manipulations of Christian motifs and sources. Michael Rosenberg's "Sexual Serpents and Perpetual Virginity" is a good example of such a study. In this article, he describes how themes of a painless birth and an intact hymen (so prevalent in Eastern Christian texts, written by Christians living in the vicinity of the Babylonian Talmud authors) are pursued in Talmudic texts from the seventh to the twelfth centuries in oblique references to Mary's immaculate conception and birth. He concludes that these responses fall into two categories: mocking anti-Marian passages and appropriations of the self-same themes for the mothers of the Jewish messiah. That is, they either reject these themes or they apply them to the mother of the Jewish messiah. Thus, the Jewish and Christian narratives dueled for priority of maternal righteousness and purity. Rosenberg sees these as evidence in both traditions of "the appeal of a strong feminine presence in a *corredemptrix* role," i.e., mothers that redeem through their procreative and sexual purity. See also Himmelfarb, "Mother of the Messiah."

58. There are also medieval rabbinic accounts of Rebecca's accidental defloration as she traveled back to Isaac after being betrothed to him. She falls from a camel after seeing Isaac for the first time and her hymen breaks. There follows a drama in which Isaac suspects Rebecca of sleeping with his servant who accompanied her on the trip. They return to the scene of the fall and Rebecca's blood is still on the ground. These accounts include all the components of the sexual dissection of the matriarchs: (self-)

defloration, suspicion of sexual immorality, physical/technical scrutiny, and vindication. See Kasher, *Torah Shelemah,* and Ginzberg, *Legends of the Jews.*

59. Note that scholars today and I, myself, in this book refer to Tamar as a Canaanite. This is the dominant scholarly position at this time, although the Hebrew Bible does not explicitly specify her ethnicity.

60. *T. Jud.* 11.1–5.

61. *T. Jud.* 12.2.

62. *Gen. Rab.* 45.4.

63. Malkiel, "Manipulating Virginity," 110–11.

64. Malkiel, "Manipulating Virginity," 111.

65. Margaliyot, *Midrash Haggadol*, 327.

66. *Gen. Rab.* 85:9–10; *t. Nid.* 2:6, cited in Malkiel, *Manipulating Virginity*, 113.

67. *b. Yebam.* 34b.

68. Kara-Ivanov Kaniel, "Myth of the Messianic Mother," 89.

CHAPTER 5

69. See n11 above.

70. Cyril of Jerusalem, *Catechesis* 12:28, PG 33:760 B–C.

71. Gregory of Nyssa, *Nat. Christi*, PG 46:1113 D–1136 B.

72. Severus of Antioch, "Homily 67," PO 8:353.

73. Damascène, Homily 103.

74. English translation of quoted verses 7–13 by Kronholm, "Holy Adultery."

75. The ark of the covenant was an ornate wooden chest that contained large stones on which God's commandments to the Jewish people were engraved. It first appears in the book of Exodus in the Hebrew Bible. The comparison of Mary to the ark establishes a metaphor: God's laws and his covenant (or connection) with the Israelites that were kept within the ark become Jesus as the new law and the new covenant with his followers that were kept within Mary.

76. The manna in the desert was a kind of heavenly food (or bread) that the Hebrew Bible God sent down each morning to the Israelites to keep them from starving as they made their way from Egypt to the promised land in Canaan.

77. Athanasius, *Hom. Pap. Turin*, 216–17.

78. While a more benign reading of these typological readings of Hebrew Bible people and events exists, viz. that the early church fathers saw Mary and Jesus as *fulfilling prophecy* rather than replacing and exceeding Israelite history and heroes, the rhetoric of the early fathers is as much, if not more, interested in the competitive advantage they constructed in these interpretations.

79. Proclus of Constantinople, Homily 5:3, PG 65:720B.

80. Chapters 2–3 in Genesis in the Hebrew Bible recount the creation and fall of the first human beings, Adam and Eve. Having completed the creation of the world, God turns to create humanity. The first man, Adam, was created out of the dust of the earth and God breathed the breath of life into his nostrils and he lived. God placed Adam in an idyllic garden, Eden, and created a "helper" to be with him out of his rib: a woman, Eve. God told them not to eat of the tree of the knowledge of good and evil at the center of the garden. A serpent comes and convinces Eve to eat the fruit because it will make her and Adam like God, knowing good and evil. Both Eve and Adam eat. They see that they are naked and clothe themselves. God comes to the garden and realizes, because of the clothes they wear, that they have eaten of the forbidden fruit and he punishes

them. Adam will labor for his living. Eve will have pain in childbirth. Finally, they both become mortal; that is, capable of dying. God tells them: "You are dust, to dust you will return." He exiles them from the garden of Eden. From this story comes the Christian doctrine of original sin. It is an etiology of human hardship and mortality.

81. As cited in McGrath, *Introduction to Christianity*, 131–32.
82. Basil of Caesarea, *Adv. Eunom.* 2:15, PG 29:601 B-C.
83. Origen, *Comm. Rom.* 3:10, PG 14:956–957.
84. Epiphanius of Salamis, *De Fide* 30, PG 43:72 B and 32; PG 43:76 A–B.
85. Basil of Caesarea, *Hom. Gen. Chr.* 3, PG 31:1464A.
86. *Prot. Jas.* 19:2 (*NT Apoc.* 1:384).
87. *Prot. Jas.* 19:3 (*NT Apoc.* 1:385).
88. *Prot. Jas.* 20:1 (*NT Apoc.* 1:385).
89. Pseudo-Chrysostom, *Hom. Annunc. Mater Dei*, PG 62:765–68.
90. Haase, "Die koptischen Quellen," 50–51.
91. Caelius Sedulis, *Carm.* 2:45–47, PL 19:596.
92. Jerome, *De Virg. Perp.* 19, PL 23:203.
93. Jerome, *De Virg. Perp.* 19, PL 23:203.
94. Jerome, *De Virg. Perp.* 19, PL 23:203.
95. Jerome, *De Virg. Perp.* 19, PL 23:203.
96. See Gambero, *Mary and the Fathers of the Church*, 209. Indeed many of the fathers' texts that I cite in this chapter appear in Gambero's survey of the church fathers' writings on Mary.
97. My discussion of these two texts by Tertullian relies, in part, on Glancy, "Law of the Opened Body," 267–288.
98. Tertullian, *Adv. Marc.* 3.11.
99. Glancy, "Law of the Opened Body," 275.
100. Tertullian, *Adv. Marc.* 4.21.
101. Glancy, "Law of the Opened Body," 275–77.
102. Glancy, "Law of the Opened Body," 275–77.
103. Tertullian, *De Carn. Christi* 4. English translation by P. Holmes, ANF 3:3–9.
104. Glancy, "Law of the Opened Body," 281.
105. Tertullian, *De Carn. Chr.* 23.1–9.
106. Origen, *Comm. Rom.* 3:10, PG 14:956–957.
107. Solberg, "Madonna, Whore,"195.
108. Solberg, "Madonna, Whore," 195–96.
109. Peter Chrysologus, *Sermon* 140:2, PL 52:576.
110. Chrysostom, *Hom. Matt.* 4:3, PG 57:43.
111. Chrysostom, *Hom. Gen.* 49:2, PG 54:446.
112. Chrysostom, *Obs. Proph.* 1:2, PG 56:166–167.
113. Pseudo-Chrysostom, *Hom. Annunc. Mater Dei*, PG 62.
114. McNabb, transl., "Ode in Honour of the Holy Immaculate Most Blessed Glorious Lady Mother of God and Ever Virgin," IX.7–11.
115. Ambrose of Milan, Epistle 42:13, PL 16:1176.
116. Gregory Nazianzen, Epistle 101, PG 37:177C–180A.
117. Rushin, "Bridge Poem," xxi–xxii.

CHAPTER 6

118. Ambrose of Milan, *De Virg.* 2:7, PL 16:220.

119. Justin, *Dial. Trypho* 67, ANF 1:231.

120. Celsus, *True Doctrine*, 58.

121. Berger, *Jewish-Christian Debate*, 41–44.

122. Cameron, "Images of Authority," 5–6.

123. Cameron, "Images of Authority," 19–20. Quoting from the Russian translation of the sermon by Laparov.

124. Trypanis, *Fourteen Early Byzantine Cantica*, 17–21.

125. Justin, *Dial. Trypho* 100, ANF 1:249. Justin's parallel between Eve and Mary almost certainly grew out of passages in the letters of Paul, the apostle, in the New Testament in which he developed a strong parallel between Adam and Christ with Christ righting the wrongs of the first man (for example, Romans 5:12, 21 and 1 Corinthians 15:21–22).

126. Luigi Gambero summarizes the logic well in "Patristic Intuitions," 87: "Recapitulation for Irenaeus means a 'summing up in Christ of all things,' from the beginning of creation. In this perspective, salvation is a second creation or a new creation, a repetition of the first one, through which God rehabilitates the earlier plan of salvation that had been suspended because of the sin committed by Adam and Eve."

127. Irenaeus, *Haer.* 3:22, PG 7:959–960.

128. Gambero, *Mary and the Fathers*, 55.

129. 1 Timothy 2:5.

130. Giamberardini, "*Sub tuum*," 343.

131. Venantius Fortunatus, *Laud. Sanct. Mar.*, PL 88: 276–284.

132. Gambero, *Mary and the Fathers*, 327.

133. Augustine, *Sermon at Denis (Sermo Denis)* 25:7.

134. Epiphanius of Salamis, *Adv. Haer.* 79:4, PG 42:745 C–D.

135. *Lumen Gentium*, 54.

136. *Lumen Gentium*, 56.

137. *Lumen Gentium*, 58.

138. *Redempt. Mater*, 1.

139. *Redempt. Mater*, 18.

140. Among many other scholars who write on such texts and their cooptation of maternity to authorize the church, two inform my analysis here: Buell, *Making Christians*, and Penniman, *Raised on Christian Milk*.

141. Irenaeus, *Haer.* 4.38, PG 7:1106.

142. Clement of Alexandria, *Paed.* 1.6 (ANF 2:220). Translation from Chambers, "Seeding as Suckling," 60.

143. *Paed.* 1.6 (ANF 2:220).

144. *Paed.* 1.6 (ANF 2:220).

145. *Paed.* 1.6 (ANF 2:218).

146. *Paed.* 1.6 (ANF 2:220).

147. Hippolytus, *On the Blessings of the Patriarchs* I, PO 27, 108–12.

148. Ephrem, *Hymn to the Virgin* 7.7–8. In *Ephrem the Syrian: Hymns*, 294–95. Translation from Brock, *Harp of the Spirit*, 48–49.

149. Leo the Great, Sermon 29:1, PL 54:227.

150. Gallagher, "Fertility rate," para. 1.

151. For the history and continued significance of the ten lost tribes of Israel in Jewish religion and culture, see "Ten Lost Tribes of Israel" in the *Encyclopedia Britannica*.

152. Ford supported the publication of a series of anti-Semitic articles in a newspaper he had purchased, *The Dearborn Independent*, penned by his protégé, William J. Cameron, who was a proponent of Anglo-Israelism. (See McFarland and Gottfried, "Chosen Ones."

153. For a more detailed account of the dissemination and widespread reception of *The Protocols*, as well as its anti-Semitic rhetoric see Wallace, *American Axis*, 13–14.

154. Flannery, *Understanding Apocalyptic Terrorism*, 148.

155. Details of this ideology from Flannery, *Understanding Apocalyptic Terrorism*, 148–150. This is a good, accessible read if you want to learn more about continued adherence to this ideology in America today and its violent potential for domestic terrorism.

156. According to Seth Jones at the Center for Strategic and International Studies, domestic terrorism is on the rise. The "incel" movement is probably the most blatant instance of domestic terrorism aimed at women. He explains that "Involuntary celibates, or incels, conduct acts of violence against women. The incel movement is composed of a loosely organized virtual community of young males. Incels believe that one's place in society is determined by physical characteristics and that women are responsible for this hierarchy. Incels identify with the writings of Elliot Rodger, who published a 133-page manifesto, titled 'My Twisted World.' In October 2015, Christopher Harper-Mercer, inspired by Rodger, killed nine people at a community college in Oregon. In November 2018, 40-year-old Scott Beierle killed two women in a yoga studio in Tallahassee, Florida, before committing suicide." This analysis and more can be found at https://www.csis.org/analysis/escalating-terrorism-problem-united-states.

157. Robertson, Mele, and Tavernise, "11 Killed in Synagogue Massacre," *New York Times*, October 27, 2018. https://www.nytimes.com/2018/10/27/us/active-shooter-pittsburgh-synagogue-shooting.html.

158. Vargas and Juárez, "El Pasoans remember."

159. Chapin, "White Nationalists."

160. Lorde, "Black Mother Woman," *Collected Poems*, 222.

Bibliography

A good number of the ancient sources cited in this book are found in scholarly collections, both in print and online. These collections are listed in the endnotes in abbreviated format and may be difficult to decipher. Here, then, are the relevant abbreviations as they appear in the endnotes, should you wish to find the complete source texts to read further on your own:

Ante-Nicene Fathers	(ANF)
Old Testament Pseudipigrapha	(OTP)
Patrologia Graeca	(PG)
Patrologia Latina	(PL)
Patrologia Orientalis	(PO)
Sources Chrétiennes	(SC)

In addition, most of the rabbinic texts, whether Mishnaic, Talmudic, Midrashic, or Commentative, may be found at www.sefaria.org, a nonprofit organization that offers free access to over three thousand years of Jewish texts. The abbreviations in the endnotes are included here in the bibliography for cross-referencing.

Ambrose of Milan. "Epistle 42: To the Most Merciful Emperor Eugenius" In vol. 16 of *Patrologia Latina*. Edited by J.-P. Migne. 217 vols. Paris, 1844–1864.

———. *On Virginity* (*De Virg.*). In vol. 16 of *Patrologia Latina*. Edited by J.-P. Migne. 217 vols. Paris, 1844–1864.

Angier, Natalie. "For Motherly X Chromosome, Gender Is Only the Beginning." *The New York Times,* May 1, 2007. www.nytimes.com/2007/05/01/science/01angi.html?ref=science.

The Ante-Nicene Fathers. Edited by Alexander Roberts and James Donaldson. 1885–1887. 10 vols. Peabody, MA: Hendrickson, 1994.

Athanasius. *Homily of the Papyrus of Turin* (*Hom. Pap. Turin*). Edited by T. Lefort. *Le Muséon: Revue d'Études Orientales* 71 (1958) 209–33.

Augustine. *Of Marriage and Concupiscence.* Translated by Peter Holmes and Robert Ernest Wallis. Revised by Benjamin B. Warfield. Updated by A. M. Overett. Savage, MN: Lighthouse Christian Publishing, 2018.

———. *Sermon at Denis*. In *Miscellanea Agostiniana: Sancti Augustini sermones post Maurinos reperti*. Edited by Germaine Morin. Vatican City: Tipografia Poiglotta Vaticana, 1930.

Basil of Caesarea. Against Eunomius (*Adv. Eunom.*). In vol. 29 of *Patrilogia Graeca*. Edited by J.-P. Migne. 162 vols. Paris, 1857–1886.

———. *Sermon on the Generation of Christ* (*Hom. Gen. Chr.*). In vol. 31 of *Patrilogia Graeca*. Edited by J.-P. Migne. 162 vols. Paris, 1857–1886.

Ben Asher, Bachya (rabbeinu). *Genesis* (*R. Bachya*). Sefaria Living Library. https://www.sefaria.org/Rabbeinu_Bahya%2C_Bereshit.19.30.2.

Ben Asher, Jacob (rabbi). *Tur HaArokh*. Sefaria Living Library. https://www.sefaria.org/Tur_HaArokh%2C_Genesis.

Ben Moses Arama, Isaac (rabbi). *Akeidat Yitzchak*. Sefaria Living Library. https://www.sefaria.org/Akeidat_Yitzchak.

Berger, David. *The Jewish-Christian Debate in the High Middle Ages: A Critical Edition of the Nizzahon Vetus*. Philadelphia: The Jewish Publication Society of America, 1979.

Brock, Sebastian P. "The Genealogy of the Virgin Mary in Sinai Syr. 16." *Scrinium* 2 (2006) 58–71.

———. *The Harp of the Spirit: Twelve Poems of Saint Ephrem*. Studies Supplementary to *Sobornost* 4. London: Fellowship of St. Alban and St. Sergius, 1975.

Buell, Denise Kimber. *Making Christians: Clement of Alexandria and the Rhetoric of Identity*. Princeton: Princeton University Press, 1999.

Caelius Sedulis. *Hymns* (*Carm.*). In vol. 19 of *Patrologia Latina*. Edited by J.-P. Migne. 217 vols. Paris, 1844–1864.

Cameron, Averil. "Images of Authority: Elites and Icons in Late Sixth-Century Byzantium." *Past and Present* 84.1 (1979) 3–35.

Carroll, James. *Constantine's Sword: The Church and the Jews: A History*. Boston: Houghton-Mifflin, 2001.

Celsus. *On the True Doctrine: A Discourse Against the Christians*. Translated by R. Joseph Hoffman. Oxford: Oxford University Press, 1987.

Chambers, Matthew J. "Seeding as Suckling: The Milk of the Father in Clement of Alexandria's *Paedagogus* I 6." Pages 59–73 in *Studia Patristica* 72. Leuven: Peeters, 2014.

Chadwick, H. "Some Reflections on the Character and Theology of the Odes of Solomon." In *Kyriakon: Festschrift Johannes Quasten*, 2 vols., edited by P. Granfield and J. A. Jungmann, 266–70. Münster: Aschendorff, 1970.

Chapin, Angelina. "How White Nationalists Weaponize Motherhood." *The Cut*, July 31, 2020. https://www.thecut.com/2020/07/sisters-in-hate-how-white-nationalists-weaponize-motherhood.html.

Chrysostom. *Eight Homilies Against the Jews* (*Adv. Jud.*). Homily 2. Fordham University Internet History Sourcebooks Project. www.fordham.edu/halsell/source/chrysostom-jews6-homily2-LOST.asp.

———. "Sermon 49 on Genesis" (*Hom. Gen.*). In vol. 54 of *Patrologia Graeca*. Edited by J.-P. Migne. 162 vols. Paris, 1857–1886.

———. "Sermon 4 on Matthew" (*Hom. Matt.*). In vol. 57 of *Patrologia Graeca*. Edited by J.-P. Migne. 162 vols. Paris, 1857–1886.

———. "Sermon 1 on the Obscurities of the [Hebrew Bible] Prophecies" (*Obs. Proph.*). In vol. 56 of *Patrologia Graeca*. Edited by J.-P. Migne. 162 vols. Paris, 1857–1886.

Clement of Alexandria. *The Instructor* (*Paed.*). In vol. 2 of *The Ante-Nicene Fathers*. Edited by Alexander Roberts and James Donaldson. 10 vols. 1885–1887.

Corrington, Gail Paterson. "The Milk of Salvation: Redemption by the Mother in Late Antiquity and Early Christianity." *Harvard Theological Review* (1989) 393–420.

Cyril of Jerusalem. *Catechesis XII*. In vol. 33 of *Patrologia Graeca*. Edited by J.-P. Migne. 162 vols. Paris, 1857–1886.

Damascène, Jean. *Homélies sur la nativité et dormition*. Sources Chrétiennes 80. Edited and translated by Pierre Voulet. Paris: Cerf, 1961.

Drijvers, Hans J. W. "The 19th Ode of Solomon: Its Interpretation and Place in Syriac Christianity." *Journal of Theological Studies* 21 (1980) 337–55.

Ephrem the Syrian. *Hymn on Virginity*. In *Ephrem the Syrian: Hymns*, 294–95. Translated by Kathleen E. McVey. New York: Paulist, 1989.

———. *Hymn to the Virgin*. In *The Harp of the Spirit: Twelve Poems of Saint Ephrem*, by Sebastian P. Brock. Studies Supplementary to *Sobornost* 4. London: Fellowship of St. Alban and St. Sergius, 1975.

Epiphanius of Salamis. *Against Heresies* (*Adv. Haer.*). In vol. 42 of *Patrologia Graeca*. Edited by J.-P. Migne. 162 vols. Paris, 1857-1886.

———. *De Fide*. In vols. 30 and 32 of *Patrologia Graeca*. Edited by J.-P. Migne. 162 vols. Paris, 1857–1886.

Epistula Apostolorum (*Ep. Apos.*). In *The Apocryphal New Testament*, edited by Montague Rhode James, 485–503. Oxford: Clarendon, 1924.

Flannery, Frances L. *Understanding Apocalyptic Terrorism: Countering the Radical Mindset*. London: Routledge, 2016.

Fonrobert, Charlotte Elisheva. "The Handmaid, the Trickster and the Birth of the Messiah: A Critical Appraisal of the Feminist Valorization of Midrash Aggada." In *Current Trends in the Study of Midrash*, edited by Carol Bakhos, 245–75. Leiden: Brill, 2006.

Gallagher, James. "Fertility rate: 'Jaw-dropping' global crash in children being born." BBC Health, July 15, 2020. https://www.bbc.com/news/health-53409521.

Gambero, Luigi. *Mary and the Fathers of the Church: The Blessed Virgin Mary in Patristic Thought*. Translated by Thomas Buffer. San Francisco: Ignatius, 1999. Orig. *Maria nel pensiero dei padri della Chiesa*. Milan: Edizione Paoline, R. S. I., 1991.

———. "Patristic Intuitions of Mary's Role as Mediatrix and Advocate: The Invocation of the Faithful for Her Help." *Marian Studies* 52 (2001) 78–101.

Genesis Rabbah ("The Great Genesis") (*Gen. Rab.*). Sefaria Living Library. https://www.sefaria.org/Bereishit_Rabbah.

Giamberardini, Gabriele. "Il *Sub tuum praesidium* e il titolo *Theotókos* nella tradizione egiziana." *Marianum* 31 (1969) 343.

Ginzberg, Louis. *The Legends of the Jews*. 7 vols. Philadelphia: Jewish Publication Society, 1909–1938.

Gregory Nazianzen. "Epistle 101: To Cledonius, Priest, Against Apollinarius." In vol. 37 of *Patrologia Graeca*. Edited by J.-P. Migne. 162 vols. Paris, 1857–1886.

Gregory of Nyssa. *Homily on the Nativity of Christ* (*Nat. Christi*). In vol. 46 of *Patrologia Graeca*. Edited by J.-P. Migne. 162 vols. Paris, 1857–1886.

Grillmeier, Aloys. *Christ in Christian Tradition: From the Apostolic Age to Chalcedon (451)*. Translated by John Bowden. Atlanta: John Knox, 1965.

Glancy Jennifer A. "The Law of the Opened Body: Tertullian on the Nativity." *Henoch* 30:2 (2008) 267–88.

Haase, Felix Artur Julius. "Die koptischen Quellen zum Konzil von Nicaea, Kap 34–35." *Studien zur Geschichte und Kultur des Altertums* 10:4 (1920).

Hannah, Darrell D. *Michael and Christ: Michael Traditions and Angel Christology in Early Christianity*. Tübingen: Mohr Siebeck, 1999.

Himmelfarb, Martha. "The Mother of the Messiah in the Talmud Yerushalmi and Sefer Zerubabbel." In *The Talmud Yerushalmi and Graeco-Roman Culture III*. Vol. 93 of Texts and Studies in Ancient Judaism, edited by Peter Schäfer and Catherine Hezser, 383–90. Tübingen: Mohr Siebeck, 1998.

Hippolytus. *On the Blessings of the Patriarchs*. In vol. 27 of *Patrologia Orientalis*. Edited and translated by Louis Mariès, et al. 49 vols. Paris: Firmin-Didot, 1954.

Irenaeus of Lyons. *Against Heresies* (*Haer.*). In vol. 7 of *Patrologia Graeca*. Edited by J.-P. Migne. 162 vols. Paris, 1857–1886.

Jerome. *The Perpetual Virginity of Mary* (*De Virg. Perp.*). In vol. 23 of *Patrologia Latina*. Edited by J.-P. Migne. 217 vols. Paris, 1844–1864.

The Jewish-Christian Debate in the High Middle Ages: A Critical Edition of the Nizzahon Vetus. Translated by David Berger. Philadelphia: JPS, 1979.

John Paul II. *Mother of the Redeemer* (*Redempt. Mater*). Vatican.va. http://www.vatican.va/content/john-paul-ii/en/encyclicals/documents/hf_jp-ii_enc_25031987_redemptoris-mater.html

Jones, Seth, Catrina Doxsee, and Nicholas Harrington. "The Escalating Terrorism Problem in the United States." https://www.csis.org/analysis/escalating-terrorism-problem-united-states.

Justin Martyr. *Dialogue with Trypho*. In vol. 1 of *The Ante-Nicene Fathers*. Edited by Alexander Roberts and James Donaldson. 10 vols. 1885–1887.

Kara-Ivanov Kaniel, Ruth "The Myth of the Messianic Mother in Jewish and Christian Traditions: Psychoanalytic and Gender Perspectives." *Journal of the American Academy of Religion* 83:1 (2014) 72–119.

Kasher, M. M. *Torah Shelemah*. 12 vols. Jerusalem: Hotzaat Beit Torah Shelemah, 1934.

Ko, Lisa. "Unwanted Sterilization and Eugenics Programs in the United States." https://www.pbs.org/independentlens/blog/unwanted-sterilization-and-eugenics-programs-in-the-united-states/.

Kristeva, Julia. "Stabat Mater." Translated by Arthur Goldhammer. *Poetics Today* 6.1–2. The Female Body in Western Culture: Semiotic Perspectives (1985) 133–152.

Kronholm, T. "Holy Adultery: The Interpretation of the Story of Judah and Tamar (Gen 38) in the Genuine Hymns of Ephraem Syrus (c. 306–373)." *Orientalia Suecana* 40 (1991) 149–63.

Leo the Great. "Sermon 29: On the Birth of the Lord." In vol. 54 of *Patrologia Latina*. Edited by J.-P. Migne. 217 vols. Paris, 1844–1864.

Lorde, Audre. "Black Mother Woman." In *The Collected Poems of Audre Lorde*, 222. New York: W. W. Norton & Company, 1997.

Malkiel, David. "Manipulating Virginity: Digital Defloration in Midrash and History." *Jewish Studies Quarterly* 13 (2006) 105–27.

Margaliyot, Mordecai, ed. *Midrash Haggadol*. Jerusalem: Mosad Haraw Kook, 1947.

McFarland, Michael, and Glenn Gottfried. "The Chosen Ones: A Mythic Analysis of the Theological and Political Self-Justification of Christian Identity." *Journal for the Study of Religion* 15:1 (2002) 125–45.

McGrath, Alister E. *An Introduction to Christianity*. Cambridge: Blackwell, 1997.

Montemurro, Beth, and Jenna Marie Siefken. "MILFS and Matrons: Images and Realities of Mothers' Sexuality." *Sexuality and Culture* 16 (2012) 366–88.

Moraga, Cherríe, and Gloria Anzaldúa, eds. *This Bridge Called My Back: Writings by Radical Women of Color.* New York: Persephone, 1981.

New Testament Apocrypha (*NT Apoc.*). 2 vols. Edited by Wilhelm Schneemelcher. Translated by R. McL. Wilson. Philadelphia: Westminster, 1963.

"Ode in Honour of the Holy Immaculate Most Blessed Glorious Lady Mother of God and Ever Virgin." Translated by Vincent McNabb. *The Journal of Christendom College* 28:1 (Summer 2003) 2–13.

Odes of Solomon (*Odes Sol.*). In vol. 2 of *Old Testament Pseudipigrapha.* 4th ed. Edited by James H. Charlesworth. New York: Doubleday, 2015.

Old Testament Pseudepigrapha. 2 vols. 4th ed. Edited by James H. Charlesworth. New York: Doubleday, 2015.

Origen of Alexandria. *Commentary on Romans* (*Comm. Rom.*). In vol. 14 of *Patrologia Graeca.* Edited by J.-P. Migne. 162 vols. Paris, 1857–1886.

Patrologia Graeca. Edited by J.-P. Migne. 162 vols. Paris, 1857–1886.

Patrologia Latina. Edited by J.-P. Migne. 217 vols. Paris, 1844–1864.

Paul VI. *Lumen Gentium* (*Light of the Nations*), 54. Vatican.va (1964). https://www.vatican.va/archive/hist_councils/ii_vatican_council/documents/vat-ii_const_19641121_lumen-gentium_en.html.

Penniman, John David. *Raised on Christian Milk: Food and the Formation of the Soul in Early Christianity.* New Haven: Yale University Press, 2017.

Peter Chrysologus. *Sermon 140: The Annunciation to the Blessed Virgin Mary.* In vol. 52 of *Patrologia Latina.* Edited by J.-P. Migne. 217 vols. Paris, 1844–1864.

Pirke d'Rabbi Eliezer ("Chapters of Rabbi Eliezer") (*Pirqe R. El.*). Sefaria Living Library. https://www.sefaria.org/Pirkei_DeRabbi_Eliezer.

Planned Parenthood. "*Roe v. Wade*: Its History and Impact." https://www.plannedparenthood.org/files/3013/9611/5870/Abortion_Roe_History.pdf.

Pseudo-Chrysostom. "Sermon on the Annunciation to the Mother of God" (*Hom. Annunc. Mater Dei*). In vol. 62 of *Patrologia Graeca.* Edited by J.-P. Migne. 162 vols. Paris, 1857–1886.

Quasten, Johannes. *Patrology.* 4 vols. Westminster: Christian Classics, 1991.

Radak (Rabbi David Kimchi). *Genesis.* Sefaria Living Library. https://www.sefaria.org/Radak_on_Genesis.

Rashi (Rabbi Shlomo ben Yitzhak). *Genesis.* Sefaria Living Library. https://www.sefaria.org/Rashi_on_Genesis.

Robertson, Campbell, Christopher Mele, and Sabrina Tavernise. "11 Killed in Synagogue Massacre; Suspect Charged With 29 Counts." https://www.nytimes.com/2018/10/27/us/active-shooter-pittsburgh-synagogue-shooting.html.

Roncace, Mark, and Deborah Whitehead. "Reading the Religious Romance: Sexuality, Spirituality, and Motherhood in the Bible and Today." In *Mother Goose, Mother Jones, Mommie Dearest: Biblical Mothers and Their Children*, edited by Cheryl A. Kirk-Duggan and Tina Pippin, 113–28. Atlanta: Society of Biblical Literature, 2009.

Rosenberg, Michael. "Sexual Serpents and Perpetual Virginity: Marian Rejectionism in the Babylonian Talmud." *The Jewish Quarterly Review* 106:4 (Fall 2016) 465–93.

Rushin, Donna Kate. "Bridge Poem." In *This Bridge Called My Back: Writings by Radical Women of Color*, edited by Cherríe Moraga and Gloria Anzaldúa, xxi–xxii. New York: Persephone, 1981.

Sanhedrin ("Assembly of Judges") (*b. Sanh.*). Sefaria Living Library. https://www.sefaria.org/Sanhedrin.69b.

Sariola, H., and A. Uutela, "The prevalence and context of incest abuse in Finland." *Child Abuse & Neglect* 20:9 (1996) 243–50.

"Sefaria: A Living Library of Jewish Texts." *www.sefaria.org*.

Sefer HaYashar: Vayera (*Sep. HaYashar*). Sefaria Living Library. https://www.sefaria.org/Sefer_HaYashar_(midrash)%2C_Book_of_Genesis%2C_Vayera.

Severus of Antioch. "Homily 67." In vol. 37 of *Patrologia Orientalis*. Paris: Firmin-Didot, 1912.

Solberg, Emma Maggie. "Madonna, Whore: Mary's Sexuality in the N-Town Plays." *Comparative Drama* 48:3 (Fall 2014) 191–219.

Stern, Alexandra Minna. *Eugenic Nation: Faults and Frontiers of Better Breeding in Modern America*. American Crossroads. Oakland, CA: University of California Press, 2015.

Stiebert, Johanna. *Fathers and Daughters in the Hebrew Bible*. Oxford: Oxford University Press, 2013.

———. "Human Conception in Antiquity: The Hebrew Bible in Context." *Theology and Sexuality* 16:3 (2010) 209–227.

Sybilline Oracles (*Sib. Or.*). Edited by J. J. Collins. In vol. 2 of *Old Testament Pseudipigrapha*. 4th ed. Edited by James H. Charlesworth. New York: Doubleday, 2015.

Tertullian. *Against Marcion* (*Adv. Marc.*). In vols. 365, 368, 399, 456, 483 of *Sources Chrétiennes*. Edited by Braun René and Claudio Moreschini. Paris: Éditions du Cerf, 1990.

———. On the Flesh of Christ (*De Carn. Christi*). In vols. 216–217 of *Sources Chrétiennes*. Edited by Mahé Jean-Pierre. Paris: Les Éditions du Cerf, 1975.

Testament of Judah (*T. Jud.*). Translated and introduced by H. C. Kee. In vol. 1 of *Old Testament Pseudipigrapha*. 4th ed. Edited by James H. Charlesworth. New York: Doubleday, 2015.

Trypanis, C. A. *Fourteen Early Byzantine Cantica*. Vienna: Wiener byzantische Studien, V, 1968.

Vargas, Brian, and Joel Angel Juárez. "El Pasoans remember victims of the Walmart shooting one year later." *The Texas Tribune*, August 3, 2020. https://www.texastribune.org/2020/08/03/el-paso-shooting-anniversary/.

Venantius Fortunatus. *In Praise of the Holy Virgin Mary, Mother of God* (*Laud. Sanct. Mar.*). In vol. 88 of *Patrologia Latina*. Edited by J.-P. Migne. 217 vols. Paris, 1844–1864.

Wallace, Max. *The American Axis: Henry Ford, Charles Lindbergh, and the Rise of the Third Reich*. New York: St. Martin's, 2003.

World Health Organization. "WHO, Child sexual abuse: a silent health emergency." Regional Office for Africa (2004). http://www.who.int/iris/handle/123456789/1878.

Yevamot ("Widows") (*b. Yebam.*). Babylonian Talmud. Sefaria Living Library. https://www.sefaria.org/Yevamot.64a.